A PRACTICAL GUIDE TO

MEDITATION
AND PRAYER

A PRACTICAL GUIDE TO
MEDITATION AND PRAYER

J. Douglas Bottorff

UNITY® Books

Unity Village, Missouri

Revised paperback edition 1995
First edition 1990

To receive a catalog of all Unity publications (books, cassettes, and magazines) or to place an order, call the Customer Service Department: 1-800-669-0282 or (816) 251-3580.

Cover design and art by R. Anthony Design Associates

The New Revised Standard Version is used for
all Bible verses unless otherwise stated.

LIBRARY OF CONGRESS CATALOGING-IN-PUBLICATION DATA
Bottorff, J. Douglas.
  A Practical Guide to Meditation and Prayer / J. Douglas Bottorff.
  p. cm.
  Includes bibliographical references.
  1. Meditation—Christianity. 2. Prayer—Christianity. 3. Unity
School of Christianity—Doctrines. I. Title.
BV4813.B64   1990
248.3—dc20   89-51877
ISBN 0-87159-036-0
Canada GST R132529033

Unity Books feels a sacred trust to be a healing presence in the world. By printing with biodegradable soybean ink on recycled paper, we believe we are doing our part to be wise stewards of our Earth's resources.

TABLE OF CONTENTS

Preface to the 1995 Edition

Since its publication in 1990, I have used *A Practical Guide to Meditation and Prayer* as the basic text for many prayer classes I have taught. The most recent of these I completed in the latter part of 1994—approximately one year prior to the publication of this second edition. Like any responsible author, every time I use this book I do so with an eye for revising it. I am happy to say that to date there is little about it I would change. *A Practical Guide to Meditation and Prayer* still represents what I believe to be an accurate presentation of the essential principles that lead to a productive and satisfying prayer life.

The practice of meditation and prayer has led me into a personal, transformative relationship with God. I am no longer hindered by superstitions, opinions, or speculation on this subject—I am free to think for myself. In addition, the practice of meditation and prayer has, among countless other things, led me to my life's companion and to my life's work. I would not have recognized either were it not for my learning to listen to and express that deep interior impulse that fuels the forward movement of my soul. So, within an inspirational context, there are practical ends to the practices described in this book. Adhering to these simple, universal Truths, Truths that have been taught by spiritual teachers throughout all time, will enable you to solve your life's problems. The faithful practice of meditation and prayer will instill in you both the vision and the means by which you are to manifest that vision. This, I believe, is what you and I are on this planet to do. My hope is that *A Practical Guide to Meditation and Prayer* can, in some way, aid you in this exciting work.

J. Douglas Bottorff
Evergreen, Colorado
March 1995

Introduction

A newly ordained minister decided to hold a garden party for selected members of his congregation whom he wanted to get to know better. The night before the party, he realized he'd forgotten to invite Mrs. Brown, an elderly charter member who also happened to be a large financial contributor to the church. Quickly, he picked up the phone to deliver the invitation personally. "I'm sorry, but you're too late, Reverend," retorted the angry Mrs. Brown. "I've already prayed for it to rain on your party!"

Isn't it interesting to observe how people view the purpose and effects prayer is supposed to have? Though we may chuckle at the vengeful attitude of Mrs. Brown, we know it is common among many who have made prayer a part of their daily habit. People often use prayer to try to get God to rain on someone's party, change the will of another, or help only their team, their country, their political party, or their stock interests. It is precisely these kinds of self-righteous attitudes that cause the thinking person to turn from prayer as a source of help in time of need, passing it off as a practice fit only for "religious hypocrites" and people of weak character.

On the path to spiritual understanding, however, no practice is more important in terms of spiritual transformation than the practices of meditation and prayer. All metaphysical systems of thought advocate the importance of engaging in these two disciplines in one form or another, and Unity is no exception. The prayer ministry of Silent Unity is considered the very heart of the Unity movement. Throughout literature and from every pulpit and platform, there are continual invitations to put prayer first in everything we undertake. Only by doing this can we truly find a sense of meaning and satisfaction in our day-to-day experience.

Because so much emphasis is placed on meditation and prayer, questions such as these frequently arise: "How do I meditate and pray?" "What should I expect to happen?" "What is the difference between meditation and prayer?" "How do I quiet my mind for meditation?" "How does prayer work, and how can I make it work for me?" "How do I know if my prayer is heard?" These and many other important questions will be raised and addressed in the pages of this book. But before we embark upon this discussion, it is important first to establish a perspective on where these practices fit into the larger scheme of things.

I do not feel it is possible to fully understand meditation and prayer unless we first understand, to some degree, our place and purpose in the cosmic scheme of things. While most people limit the practice of prayer to the realm of temporal needs, it is, in the highest sense, the means by which we are to evolve the attributes of God and experience permanent advancement of the soul. In Part One of this book, "Laying the Foundation," my intent is to put our relationship with the Infinite into a perspective that not only lays the groundwork on *how* to meditate and pray, but also conveys an understanding of *why* we meditate and pray. When we have a sense of our place and purpose in relation to the whole, our meditation and prayer work will be more effective.

Parts Two and Three explain the theory and practice of meditation and prayer, offering some practical explanations of their functions as well as some simple steps for their practice. Part Four offers some suggestions on how prayer might be applied in the areas of healing, prosperity, and relationships. In the concluding section of Part Four, I present some thoughts on growth dynamics, using the biblical account of the Cain and Abel story as a framework. It is helpful to understand the inner forces that seem to work against our desire to grow spiritually so we may be prepared to meet successfully the challenges that confront us on our path.

This book is by no means presented as the "last word" on meditation and prayer. I do, however, believe it offers some unique, challenging, and practical insights into this very important subject. I hope that the benefits you receive from reading it are equal to the benefits I have received in preparing and presenting it to you.

PART I

Laying the Foundation

1

Cooperating With the Creative Flow

In this broad earth of ours,
Amid the measureless grossness and the
    slag,
Enclosed and safe within its central heart,
Nestles the seed perfection.

By every life a share or more or less,
None born but it is born, conceal'd or
    unconceal'd the seed is waiting.
               —Walt Whitman[1]

    The natural rhythm of life orchestrates and harmonizes every aspect of the manifest world. This rhythm is a "seed perfection" permeating and governing the unfoldment of things. Everywhere in nature, we see checks and balances that assure orderly progression of the creative flow. When one species becomes numerous enough to pose a threat to its shared environment, the predator of that species increases also. When the preyed-upon species declines, the predatory species declines accordingly. As harsh as nature's economic structure seems to be, it has successfully carried on the process of our planetary evolution for millions of years. Detecting harmony in nature is not difficult. If we are not patient enough to observe the symbiotic relations existing among the individual expressions of life, we can read about them or watch on our television sets the fruits of countless nature studies that biologists, naturalists, paleontologists, botanists, and others have provided for the general public. As these studies repeatedly reveal, the attention nature gives to balance, survival, and perpetuation of each species is astounding.

However, when we come to the world of the human species, balance and harmony are not always so evident. It is tempting to define humanity only in terms of its manifestations of selfishness, greed, territorialism, and racism. There are times when it is not difficult to share the sentiment of George Bernard Shaw when he wrote, "Only on paper has humanity yet achieved glory, beauty, truth, knowledge, virtue, and abiding love."[2]

Like the captain of a certain police force, we may have developed a pessimistic attitude toward human nature. The station had been quiet most of the week, and the detectives had spent a great deal of their time playing cards. In the height of his boredom, one of the officers grumbled, "What a boring job! No fights, no thefts, no riots, no murders, no nothin'." "Rest easy," said the captain. "Things will break soon. You just gotta have faith in human nature." Certainly there are grounds upon which to base this attitude, for it is true we have evolved to the extreme point where it is possible, by our own hand, to wipe all traces of life, human and other, from the face of this planet, to bring to an abrupt halt in a matter of hours what it has taken nature millions of years to achieve.

Human beings, however, do not operate outside the

realm of nature. Astronomer Fred Hoyle pointed this out in his book, *Frontiers of Astronomy*: "Our everyday experience even down to the smallest details seems to be so closely integrated to the grand scale features of the Universe that it is wellnigh impossible to contemplate the two being separated."[3] We are an integral part of nature, and if, as scientists believe, we have been around for at least the last four million years, it would be extremely difficult to think that we are the blundering fools some would have us believe we are. "With considerable confidence," wrote Kenneth F. Weaver in an article for *National Geographic*, "scientists are now tracing our lineage as bipedal creatures back at least four million years. And if certain fossil fragments from Kenya are hominid, the lineage may go back to five million or more."[4] It is more likely that those who live in perpetual fear of our demise do not see that evolution occurs on what often seems to be a trial-and-error basis. Even in this nuclear age, when our childlike hands and minds are probing into areas that seem to threaten the very fabric of our morality and reaching into unknown forces that can be both incredibly destructive and incomprehensibly beneficial, our rate of growth continues to increase on all fronts.

So far has the human race come that the fate of all species, including our own, rests in our hands. This has become increasingly apparent by the fact that we are intervening with and taking over the management of other species. Experts in wildlife management are now predicting the time is coming when all wildlife will be under the direct management of humankind. It would seem that, little by little, we are moving closer to that seat reserved for us at the right hand of God. Our growth carries with it undreamed-of responsibilities and implications that can sometimes frighten, sometimes anger, but more often inspire us with awe if we make an effort to keep our minds forward-looking. We would do well to share in Paul's vision when he wrote: "For the creation waits with eager longing for the revealing of the children of God ... that the creation itself will be set free from its bondage to decay and will obtain the freedom of the glory of the children of God" (Rom. 8:19, 21).

There is order in the way our species is unfolding, and we can dare say it is divine order. Each of us is here for a purpose, a purpose important to the grand scheme of things. So great is this purpose and our reason for existence that we, as individuals, will probably never fully grasp its scale. Yet we can know our place in this scheme, and we can learn to do our part in carrying it forward. We can consciously cooperate with infinite Intelligence, Power, Love, Harmony, and Order, this force we have labeled "God," and daily carry out its desire and purpose in our lives.

❧ 2 ❧

What Is Your Purpose?

What is your purpose in life? Have you ever really thought about this in relation to the big picture? Because so much emphasis is placed on the development of intellectual and physical skills in our society, you may have defined your purpose, as most people have, according to how adept you are in these areas. After all, authority and expertise are often determined by the number and kinds of degrees a person has listed after his or her name. And from the standpoint of physical development, our professional athletes command some of the grandest salaries in America.

Do you think your purpose is to be an architect, a writer, a schoolteacher, a plumber, a computer programmer, a good mother, father, son, or daughter? While all these are important roles you may play, areas of service to others in which you may make a marvelous contribution to our society or even the world at large, they are secondary to your true purpose in life. If you consider your purpose to be centered in any of these areas, the time will come when you will have no sense of purpose at all. You may retire, the kids grow up, parents pass on; any number of things can happen to remove the supposed object of your purpose, and with this removal comes the removal of a reason to live a creatively happy life.

Your purpose has to be based on a factor that will always be relevant, and the only thing you have that you will always have is your spirituality. You have intelligence and you are clothed with a body, but you are primarily a spiritual being. As a spiritual being you have a purpose, and when that purpose begins to dawn on you, you will carry it into your chosen fields of expression, whatever they may be, bringing a depth of meaning that will make your life worth living, whatever you are doing.

Understanding what this purpose is will clarify all foggy areas in your life. It will especially clarify the subjects we are dealing with in this book, meditation and prayer. The reason meditation sometimes seems difficult and even unproductive is that it is often practiced only to relax the mind and body rather than to also tap the inner spiritual resources. Prayer, too, is often misdirected because, more often than not, it is practiced solely in response to some mental, emotional, or physical desire or need. When your true purpose is understood, the reasons you meditate and pray will change dramatically.

How can we best define your purpose as a spiritual being? In simple terms we can state it thus: As a spiritual being, your purpose is to express the attributes of God in everything you do.

This statement may require some thoughtful consideration, for on the surface it may sound like an oversimplification. But you are happy and fulfilled to the degree you are involved in expressing the attributes of God. Why? Because some of the attributes of God are love, life, peace, joy, success, harmony, freedom, prosperity, wholeness, fulfillment, intelligence, enthusiasm, security, and power. Do these not comprise the essence of what you are looking for in everything you do? Do you know why you spend so much time looking for these qualities in people, places, and things? Because they are the very elements that compose your true identity, and your desire to experience their external counterparts is really the bubbling forth of God's desire to express them through you.

It would be impossible to desire to express any of these qualities as deeply and as universally as we do without our already being connected to them in some intimate way. While the feeling that we lack any of these qualities usually sparks an all-out search in the outer world of things, this sense of lack is only a signal to us that it is time to express a broader and deeper range of God's attributes in our lives. As Meister Eckhart wrote: "One must not always think so much about what one should do, but rather what one should be."[5] Herein lies the key to finding true fulfillment and satisfaction.

The first place these attributes of God must be expressed is within our consciousness. Emerson wrote: "A deep insight will always, like Nature, ultimate its thought in a thing. As soon as a man masters a principle and sees his facts in relation to it, fields, waters, skys, offer to clothe his thought in images."[6] The building of an internal foundation of consciousness always precedes the demonstration of its external equivalent. You will never see anyone sustain a lifestyle, whether it be one of poverty or prosperity, sickness or health, struggle or harmony, that is not an extension of his or her consciousness.

To get in touch with your sense of purpose, you may find it helpful to speak the following words: *As an expression of God, I now let God's infinite qualities shine through me in all I do. I am blessed with a sense of wholeness and harmony. Thank You, God.*

⫸ 3 ⫷

You Are an Individualized Expression of God

In the writings of metaphysical Christianity, we teach that each person is an individualized expression of God. Here we are talking about you as a spiritual being, not simply a mental and physical being. The intellect and body, which most people mistakenly use as their basis for identification, are the outer, ever-changing, disposable garments of your real Self. Your spiritual Self, your true Self, is an individualization of God, containing all the potentialities of Being. As such, you are the "image of God" (Gen. 1:27). The analogy most frequently drawn by Truth teachers is that of the drop of water taken from the ocean. The drop contains all the attributes of the ocean but it is not all the ocean is. It is an individualization of the ocean.

To understand this analogy, we cannot think of God as a powerful old man sitting on a throne in the sky somewhere. Dr. H. Emilie Cady shares the following enlightened description of God, which is also the basis from which the term is used in this book:

> God is Spirit, or the creative energy that is the cause of all visible things. God as Spirit is the invisible life and intelligence underlying all physical things. There could be no body, or visible part, to anything unless there were first Spirit as creative cause.
>
> God is not a being or person having life, intelligence, love, power. God is that invisible, intangible, but very real, something we call life. God is perfect love and infinite power. God is the total of these, the total of all good, whether manifested or unexpressed.[7]

As a spiritual being, you are an individualization of the whole; therefore, wholeness is your divine birthright.

❧ 4 ❧

Why Did God
Individualize as Us?

To understand our purpose in this intimate relationship with God as well as the reason for our existence, it is necessary to ask why God, or "the creative energy that is the cause of all visible things," individualized as us in the first place.

The soul, from a spiritually ideal point of view, is intended to be the transformational medium God has created and uses to convert the unexpressed divine potential into unlimited, *manifest* possibilities. By continually individualizing as the spiritual basis for an ever-growing number of new souls and endowing each one with the ability to unfold a unique combination of divine characteristics through the ability to think creatively, God is able to carry out indefinitely the process of self-expression through the manifest world. Without this ability to individualize and diversify as human beings, God would remain materially quiescent and would, therefore, be unable to fully express the divine potential. Diversification through individualization is God's method of attaining unlimited expression. You and I are the products of this cosmic methodology.

For the sake of drawing a parallel, in a musical composition each note represents an individualized expression of music. The diversity of notes available allows music to be expressed in an unlimited number of ways. Were there just one note available, music's unlimited possibilities could not be addressed and would, therefore, remain untapped potential. As it is, the unlimited combination of notes available has placed the expression of music in a category that defies definition.

The human race, in a sense, is a great musical composition. Every individual represents one musical note, one facet of God in expression. Every person is an important factor in this great symphony, for each provides a tone, a dynamic, a quality whose absence would render the composition incomplete. That the race is not fully reflecting what we conceive as the true nature of God simply indicates the symphony is still being written; this will probably always be true, for the possibilities for divine expression are limitless.

We are uniquely endowed with the same divine capability of self-expression that God is. As spiritual beings, you and I "individualize" our minds into specific ideas, creating *compositions of consciousness* that allow us to expand indefinitely in the direction of our choice. The ability to diversify in the way we express ideas indicates that we are expected to play a conscious and directive role in the course of our personal evolution. It is not intended to happen by chance or to be directed from a force outside ourselves. Our deepest desire, a desire infused into the very fabric of our being from our cosmic Source, is to be free. In cooperation with God, we are continuously seeking, consciously and unconsciously, to achieve the combination of ideas in our consciousness that will progressively allow us to move into this state.

Perpetual expansion and movement are universal tendencies shared by all aspects of the cosmos, for they can be detected in the microscopic world of subatomic particles as well as the macroscopic world of the galaxies. In his book *The Tao of Physics*, Dr. Fritjof Capra writes:

> The tendency of particles to react to confinement with motion implies a fundamental "restlessness" of matter which is characteristic of the subatomic world. In this world, most of the material particles are bound to the molecular, atomic, and nuclear structures, and therefore are not at rest but have an inherent tendency to move about—they are intrinsically restless....
>
> When we study the universe as a whole, with its millions of galaxies, we have reached the largest scale of space and time; and again, at that cosmic level ... it is expanding! This has been one of the most important discoveries in modern astronomy.[8]

God is trying to do through you what you are trying to do through your creations—attain unlimited expression. This perpetual, divine desire in you accounts for the reason you are "intrinsically restless," why, as Walt Whitman so beautifully put it:

> You but arrive at the city to which you were
> destin'd, you hardly settle yourself to

satisfaction before you are call'd by an
irresistible call to depart,
You shall be treated to the ironical smiles and
mockings of those who remain behind
you,
What beckonings of love you receive you
shall only answer with passionate kisses
of parting,
You shall not allow the hold of those who
spread their reach'd hands toward you.[9]

The only force in this universe that can ever prevent
us from continually moving toward the goal of unlimited expression is our own complacency. Even to this,
our knee will eventually bow (see Isaiah 45:23). As we
come to understand our wonderful place and purpose
in this context, we begin to cooperate with God to
bring our creations into alignment with the divine purpose and in so doing we attain our deepest desires.

The following words may go a long way in helping
you become consciously established in God's purpose
for you: *Thank You, God, for using me to fulfill Your
wonderful purpose. I am open, receptive, and obedient to
Your divine plan for my life.*

❧ 5 ❧

A Divine Mission

Think of yourself as being on a divine mission. Every moment can present a new and exciting challenge, the challenge of discovering and expressing some new level of yourself and God. Does a situation seem to have you hemmed in? Are you frustrated by apparently immovable obstacles in your life? Are you feeling the need to develop or deepen a relationship of some kind? Then your mission is to take these signals of lack that come into your awareness from somewhere in your own consciousness and start transforming them from the inside out. Your mission is to lay hold of and evolve God's characteristics through your consciousness, your body, and everything you do, to make your life "on earth as it is in heaven" (Mt. 6:10). In other words, your mission, your purpose for existence, your reason for being where you are in life is the same as the mission Jesus stated for himself when he stood before Pilate: "For this I was born, and for this I came into the world, to testify to the truth" (Jn. 18:37). You are to bear witness to the Truth of Being, to demonstrate in the visible plane that which is true on the invisible plane, and you are fulfilled to the degree that you do this.

This affirmative statement may serve to remind you of what your mission is: *Today, in every situation, I choose to bear witness to the truth by expressing the love, life, peace, and enthusiasm of God! Thank You, God.*

❧ 6 ❧

God's World and the World of Consciousness

It is important here to make a distinction between God's world and our world. While in Truth we know there is only one world, God's world, we need to understand that both as a race and as individuals we are not fully reflecting the underlying realities of God. This should almost go without saying, yet we need to make a clear distinction because confusion arises in at least two areas if we do not.

One area of confusion is found in the attitude that looks for God to intervene in world affairs as well as personal situations. Have you heard people wonder aloud why God did not do something about world conditions? Have you asked God to intervene in some personal situation? I'm sure most of us have. But God does not intervene in world affairs or personal situations any more than air can intervene and keep people from holding their breath. The world God beholds is already perfect, and God cannot "intervene" because God is *already* fully involved in it. From the standpoint of the Infinite, there is no need to correct anything. There is only a need to continually evolve mechanisms capable of supporting the perpetual expression of the infinite potential of Being.

This may be difficult to comprehend when we have spent a lifetime conceiving of God as a powerful, all-knowing, warriorlike Being enthroned in the sky, capable of defeating all enemies opposed to His will. But God's will has never once been thwarted by any aspect of creation. God is not a reactor to conditions, but rather an actor, or, as Dr. Cady put it, the "creative cause" of things.

On the other hand, there is no doubt that we have created a world that needs much correction, mainly because our sense of purpose is centered in the superficial realm of life instead of being grounded in spiritual reality. Rather than explore and change our sense of purpose and expand our limited relationship with the Infinite, we have invented and called upon a "god" whom we have come to believe lives outside our world (and in a very real sense, does) to correct the mistakes this false sense of purpose and lack of spiritual understanding produce. When there is no response to our cries for help, we feel it is because God has either become hard of hearing or is mad at us again. We need to do some rethinking in this area.

The other area of confusion is found in the attitude that says, "This is God's world and everything in it is perfect, including the struggle, pain, and limitation I am going through. It is all good." Again, a distinction between God's world and ours will clear up this confusion. Struggle, pain, and limitation are not a part of God's plan. We experience them when we try to attain fulfillment in a way that is contrary to divine law, that is, when we seek to bring our good from the outside in, rather than express it from the inside out. It is true that hard experiences can lead us, through deduction, to a greater understanding of divine law, but to say that we *need* hard experiences to develop this understanding is a false assumption. These limitations exist in the realm of human perception, not God's world. The closer we get to God in consciousness, the more our world becomes harmonized with God's world and the fewer hardships we experience. Some declare that all things that happen to them in life are good; therefore, they are not too choosy about the quality of their lives. It is one thing to say that all things are good, but quite another to say that there is good in all things. I know a man whose life is in constant turmoil and yet he displays an optimistic attitude that it is all good. There is nothing good about the turmoil he is going through, however, unless he begins to see in himself the cause for the turmoil. As he sees this and changes the patterns in his consciousness that produce the problems, he will begin to derive the good from the tumultuous conditions and will be lifted into a level where these conditions do not exist. The good to be found in any condition is *greater spiritual growth and understanding*. When that good is attained, it is reflected as harmony in outer conditions; if not, there is little or no value derived from the struggle.

It is a little like the old man who had a habit of picking up and examining everything he saw. This habit annoyed the local blacksmith, for the man would often pick things up, look them over, and put them in a different place, making it sometimes difficult to find them again. One day, while the blacksmith was shoeing a horse, he saw the man coming across the street to his shop. He quickly dipped the red-hot horseshoe in water and laid it in an obvious place for the man to see. Sure enough, the man greeted the blacksmith, saw that he was shoeing a horse, and walked right over and picked up the hot shoe. Quickly he laid it down.

"What's the matter?" the blacksmith asked, amused.

"Nothin's the matter," replied the man. "It just don't take me no time a'tall to look at a horseshoe."

In other words, there is nothing particularly good about picking up a hot horseshoe. You can get good out of the experience, however, if you learn not to do it again.

Perhaps these words can help you become established in an awareness of the idea being discussed here: *God's perfect harmony is now expressed in my world. I release all sense of hardship and struggle, remembering that God is my gentle and loving teacher and that all is well. Thank You, God.*

❧ 7 ❧

Our World Is Our Consciousness

The world in which we live is a product of our consciousness. In fact, it is our consciousness. You and I rarely experience the full potential of any event. We experience our feelings, our interpretation of the event. If we experienced the full potential of any event, we would always experience limitless bliss and unfathomable fulfillment because God is fully involved in every facet of expressed life. Were this involvement understood and experienced, we would have absolutely no consciousness of limitation of any kind. As Charles Burchfield, the American painter, said, "There is nothing commonplace in the world except the mental attitude of man."[10] It is not surprising that a painter whose eye is trained to see the multiple hues and interactions of color and objects would make such an observation. The casual observation most of us use sees a blue sky, green trees, and a brown field, as in the simplistic watercolor painting of a child; the seasoned artist uses a multitude of color combinations to express on canvas the delicate yet intelligently intentional balance of color and form he or she sees in the same scene.

Why leave the rapture produced by close observation to the artists of the world? All that God is, is accessible to us in everything we do if we will develop the eye to see it. Within the realm of our consciousness, not God's reality, there exist ideas of limitation, blocks that keep us from seeing and feeling beauty all around us. Because of this, and because our feelings are closed off to God's presence, good appears to be absent. Our reaction to this perception is responsible for creating much of the turmoil we go through in life. It is wonderful to know that we can do something about it.

In the same way, the relationship we have with each person with whom we associate is a product of our consciousness. If this were not true, all persons would appear to us as they are in Truth—Christs, sons or daughters of the living God. As it is, we see personality flaws: bad habits, fears, and selfishness in most people we meet. Why? Not because this is all there is to the people we meet but because we are seeing through a level of our own consciousness in which these things exist. In other words, we see in others what is in ourselves. We are not seeing from a God-centered state in which our eyes are too pure to behold iniquity.

Allow me to make a slight diversion here by saying that this does not mean that we are to close our eyes and blindly subject ourselves to the demands of negative people. It is even written of Jesus that he did "not entrust himself to them, because he knew all people and needed no one to testify about anyone; for he himself knew what was in everyone" (Jn. 2:24-25). There are those who have not consciously made their connection with God as their unlimited source and will attempt to use you to fulfill their selfish ends if you allow it. Spiritual discernment does not cause us to overlook this fact. In her book *Picasso,* Gertrude Stein writes of an incident in which she asked artist Henri Matisse if he viewed a tomato in the way an artist would when he ate one. "No," the artist replied, "when I eat a tomato I look at it the way anyone else would. But when I paint a tomato, then I see it differently."[11] It is important for us to be able to view people with this same kind of flexibility and discernment; to be able to see what they are in potential but not be blind to what they are demonstrating. A good friend once said, "All people have the Christ within them. Some are just able to hide it better than others."

We are still on solid spiritual ground when we can permit others to demonstrate in their lives what they wish, yet retain the right to decide whether or not we will allow them to demonstrate it in ours.

One of the reasons we are not always quick to invite the negative behavior of others out of our lives is that we see negative behavior in ourselves, and feel that we have no right to judge another in this way. We may even be hounded by Jesus' challenging words: "Why do you see the speck in your neighbor's eye, but do not notice the log in your own eye? Or how can you say to your neighbor, 'Let me take the speck out of your eye,' while the log is in your own eye? You hypocrite, first take the log out of your own eye, and then you will see clearly to take the speck out of your neighbor's eye" (Mt. 7:3-5).

Notice that Jesus' statement has to do with our tendency to want to change people to conform to our expectations and standards. To attempt to do this is somewhat hypocritical, for none of us can honestly say that we have life totally figured out. Certainly we can help those who feel we can offer them something of value, but the moment we begin to try to change people because we think we know what is best for them, we open ourselves to having our own flaws exposed.

We are not talking about changing others here. We are talking about changing ourselves. If people want to spread negativity throughout the lives of others, that is between them and the people they affect. If they want to spread their negativity in your life, you are in no way obligated to allow it. You do not have to eliminate all the flaws in yourself before you begin making decisions on what you will and will not permit others to do with you. If a person's behavior has the effect of degrading the quality of life you are trying to achieve, you have first of all to acknowledge what in you is permitting this to happen. Second, you have to do something about it. This does not mean you have to pass condemnatory judgment on the person. It is like a friend once said, "You can appreciate a skunk for the beautiful animal that it is, but you do not have to allow it to live under your house."

So, there is your world, the world as you see it through *your* consciousness, and there is God's world, the underlying reality of Absolute Good that is forever gently asserting itself, yet never forcing itself, into greater levels of expression through every facet of creation. Your work is to bring your world steadily into alignment with the world of God, to coordinate your personal purpose with the divine purpose, and to begin within yourself to unleash your unlimited potential through every facet of your creation. How is this done?

By peering directly into the mechanics of the creative process as it occurs within you and receiving firsthand knowledge from your Creator on how it is all done. Your ticket into this wonderful world of creation is obtained through the practice of meditation.

Before we move on to the subject of meditation, let us review some of the highlights of this first part. You are an integral part of the universe; your purpose is to express more of the attributes of God in everything you do. God has individualized as you so that a new and unique facet of divinity can express through the manifest world, insuring unlimited divine expression. You are endowed with the same creative ability God has. Therefore, you are capable of carrying out the divine desire for unlimited expression in your own original way. Your desire for greater good is really God desiring to express through you and is a promise that that which you deeply desire—a rich, abundant, free life—is yours by your divine birthright. The way to achieve it is to develop a consciousness of it. From this consciousness of abundance springs forth a quality of life you know in your heart of hearts is possible to attain.

PART II

Meditation

❧ 1 ❧

What Is Meditation?

What exactly is meditation? The answer you get will depend on whom you ask. Ask the Eastern yogi and you may be told that it is a discipline to put you in touch with the essence of all life. Ask a Western holistic doctor and he or she may tell you it is deep physical and mental relaxation. Ask a fundamentalist Christian and you may be told that it is a heathen practice to be avoided at all costs. Ask certain others and they may describe meditation as a dreamy state that usually precedes sleep and is often experienced in church.

The word *meditation* is a general term that can be and is used to describe a variety of mental and spiritual exercises. Of the several definitions found in the dictionary for the word *meditate*, the two that best suit our purposes here are "to focus one's thoughts" and "to engage in contemplation or reflection." And yet the results we seek in meditation transcend both focalization of thought and contemplation, for we seek to penetrate a realm beyond these usual functions of mind.

In the writings of Unity School of Christianity, the state of consciousness required to enter this realm is usually identified as "the silence." Charles Fillmore called the silence "a state of consciousness entered into for the purpose of putting man in touch with Divine Mind so that the soul may listen to the 'still small voice.' "[12] Through the superconscious level of mind, you experience the deeper part of yourself that is directly connected with the Infinite. From this vantage point you become less a thinker and more a beholder. The continual chatter of the thinking mind is silenced, giving way to the rejuvenating spring of pure, unadulterated life.

In biblical terms, this experience could be referred to as the baptism of the Holy Spirit, though it may not be as dramatic as the baptism received by the disciples on the day of Pentecost (Acts 2:1-4). This phrase is certainly appropriate when we consider the meaning of these familiar words. Baptism indicates an immersion or a cleansing. The word *holy* is derived from the old English word *halig* which is akin to the old English word *hal* meaning whole. The baptism of the Holy Spirit, then, can be called the immersion or the merging of individual mind with universal Mind and the realization of the wholeness and omnipresence of Spirit. Initially, the individual experiences an inner transcendence of which, prior to the experience, he or she was totally unaware. Where before there may have been a sense of separation from God and other expressions of life, now all is seen as one. As the experience deepens through further exploration, the individual centers more of his or her patterns of thought in this transcendent realm and the consciousness is raised.

The story of Jacob fleeing the wrath of his brother Esau dramatically depicts his baptism of the Holy Spirit in a dream. When he awakens from sleep he says, "Surely the Lord is in this place—and I did not know it!... How awesome is this place! This is none other than the house of God, and this is the gate of heaven" (Gen. 28:16-17). How true this is! It is no wonder that this baptism has such a dramatic impact on a person who has spent a lifetime thinking of God as up in the sky somewhere. Jacob named the spot where he had this awakening *Bethel*, which means "house of God." So it is with everyone who is baptized by the Holy Spirit. We realize that we have lived in the house of God all our lives and we knew it not.

One of the turning points in my spiritual career came during a time of deep frustration. I remember waking up one morning feeling spiritually empty (as I had for some time), so I picked up a book by Charles Fillmore and began to read. Beautiful as the words on those pages were, their effect was mocking and antagonizing instead of uplifting. I wanted to be what those words described, but it seemed the harder I tried the emptier I felt inside. In a moment of anger, I threw the book down and said to God, "If You want me to learn all this stuff, then You're going to have to show me, because I'm tired of trying to do it all myself!"

There was no reply. All day I felt mad at God for giving me a vision that seemed impossible to reach. That night I was getting ready for bed and a strange thing happened. I was sitting on the edge of the bed when something in my mind suddenly opened and I could perceive a grand scheme. Everything was beautiful and in its proper place. Deep waves of love and the feeling of total acceptance rushed through me. I felt a level of contentment with myself and my surroundings that I had never felt. I could see the infinite nature of all things, animate and inanimate, and it was wondrous. A knowing came to me that said, "Do not be concerned about your life, for there is a plan for you." I felt this message was not to me alone, but to all who could receive it. In tears and total release I whispered, "Let it be that others can see what I am seeing now."

I believe this experience empowered me to eventually make the decision to enter the ministry. There I could see that what I had read about and suspected was real, yet so different than I had imagined! How could it be put into words on paper? How could it be grasped by the intellectual mind? I felt deep appreciation, gratitude, and respect for those who had tried.

The Christian fundamentalist typically sees the baptism of the Holy Spirit as a onetime event in which the initiate makes "a decision for Christ." How much of this decision is emotionalism and how much is actually a cosmic awareness is difficult to say. No doubt it varies from case to case. Obviously, the individual experiences a transcendence of some sort. Those whom I have had the opportunity to counsel on the subject tend to report it in retrospect as an emotional experience brought on by their own desire and the expectations of their peers. This is what I experienced in the church in which I grew up. I had been baptized and "saved," yet still felt Sunday after Sunday that the minister was making the altar call for me. Confused by my feelings, I asked the pastor one Sunday afternoon if I should come up again. He said I had already been saved so it would not be necessary. I still did not feel very saved because I continued to believe that he was offering the invitation to me and that Jesus was speaking to my heart. I feel that Jesus was.

The metaphysical Christian's perspective of the baptism of the Holy Spirit is that it is not a onetime event, but rather a process. We are not just "born again," as the experience might well be referred to, but again and again. Some persons pattern their expectations according to the account in Acts that baptism is always accompanied by speaking messages of Truth in strange tongues: "All of them were filled with the Holy Spirit and began to speak in other languages, as the Spirit gave them ability" (Acts 2:4). I have always felt that true spiritual baptism enables an individual to speak the Truth in plain English, or whatever language he or she is familiar with. Unity minister and author Bill Fischer called spiritual baptism "a prayer experience with Spirit, an intimate dialogue between an individual and God."[13] In any event, I am calling the process of reaching this state, the process of meditation.

Having established that your purpose in life is to express all the attributes of God in everything you do, it is important for you to know what God's attributes are. I have already listed a few, but as far as you are concerned, these may appear as just words on paper. You may want to silence your preconceptions of these words and have a firsthand experience with God. So the purpose of meditation is simply this: Meditation is the process that brings you into direct contact with attributes of God.

You can never understand your spiritual purpose unless you see for yourself what lies beyond the veil of surface level thoughts. As you penetrate this veil, you will know your purpose, not because you read about it and believed it, but because you have seen for yourself.

English philosopher and economist John Stuart Mill said: "There are many truths of which the full meaning cannot be realized until personal experience has brought it home."[14] This is certainly true of the "truths" revealed in quiet meditation. People often get into the study of Truth and the practice of meditation as a means of solving temporal problems. Nothing less than a direct experience with the qualities of pure Being will provide you with the incentive and enthusiasm necessary to continuously expand your spiritual horizons. To know God for the sake of knowing God, you have to know why you seek what you seek.

Meditation tunes you in to what we might call a life signal being sent to you from the Infinite. This is an important concept to consider because it frees you from the thought that you have to get God's attention before He will respond. The communication lines are already open. You already have God's attention and, in fact, are the manifestation of God-Mind concentrated in the place where you are. All you have to do is learn to become sensitive to the broadcast, to "tune in" to an impulse that has been within you all along. This is especially important if you have believed your relationship with God has been damaged or severed as the result of sin. While sin, in whatever way you define it, can cause a sense of separation, nothing can separate you from God. God cannot behold you as a sinner nor have any sense of condemnation for you whatsoever; however, because there is a difference in your concept of the world and God's reality, you may believe you are condemned. Your practice of meditation will gradually lift you out of this world of misconceptions and into

God's Truth. In God's Truth, you are without sin.

Perhaps these words can help you begin to break any bonds your concept of sin may have you in: *I am now free from all sin and punishment. In God's perfect love I am free to begin anew to express the unlimited beauty of my spirit. Thank You, God!*

❧ 2 ❧

How God Communicates

This life signal is what may be called a direct impression of God. All of God's attributes, which metaphysical Christianity refers to as divine ideas, are being pressed in upon you at this very moment. You may think of all of God's attributes as being present in the same way all the colors of the rainbow are present in white light. When you allow the light to pass through a prism, the various colors, or attributes, become visible. You and I are a kind of prism through which the pure, white light of God shines and reveals what Charles Fillmore taught were the twelve attributes: will, faith, understanding, imagination, zeal, power, love, wisdom, order, strength, renunciation, and life. Most people equate the presence of God's attributes to certain external conditions which they feel need to be present before that attribute can be experienced. If a person they love, for instance, is not present, they feel that love is not in their lives. If they have no cash in their wallets, they feel there is a lack of substance and an inability to appropriate it. If conditions appear chaotic, they feel there is an absence of peace. But love, substance, and peace are omnipresent and can be experienced when we practice spiritual discipline. Through our spiritual faculties, all the attributes of God are present and accessible at all times, and in whatever quantity and quality we accept them. If we choose not to accept them by not practicing our meditation and allowing ourselves to be distracted by appearances, or if we believe they can be present one day and gone the next, then this absence will appear to be real.

Awakening to this realm of God's divine attributes may require a major shift in perception, and frankly, accomplishing this shift is initially no easy matter. Because our connection with God is an inner one (by "inner" we mean the inner realms of consciousness, not necessarily a place inside the body), it would seem almost paradoxical that a number of problems confront us in achieving this shift. Why would it be difficult to re-establish this contact? Charles Fillmore, co-founder of the Unity movement, probably explained it best with this analogy: God to us is like water to a fish. The fish lives in the water all its life but it has probably never seen the water. Likewise, the emphasis we have placed on developing a strong intellect and a firm orientation around external conditions has produced a level of consciousness that is insensitive to the finer realms of Spirit. Again, Fritjof Capra writes: "Because our representation of reality is so much easier to grasp than reality itself, we tend to confuse the two and to take our concepts and symbols for reality."[15] We see but do not *see*. We hear but do not *hear*.

❧ 3 ❧

Obstacles to Meditation

The biggest obstacle you will face in entering the silence through meditation is your own busy mind. Attempts to focus the mind inward can quickly be thwarted by the intrusion of a multitude of unconnected thoughts of the most trivial nature. In the beginning, one has to be extremely patient with the process and learn how to deal effectively with the undisciplined, externally oriented mind. Your power to concentrate, however, is much greater than you may think, for, as English lexicographer and author Samuel Johnson pointed out: "When a man knows he is to be hanged in a fortnight, it concentrates his mind wonderfully."[16] When you have the desire and commitment to focus your mind in a certain direction, you can do it.

Another obstacle you may face is the tendency to search out an experience with God. This probably relates to the need to know all the facts before we have a new experience of any kind. If we have never done anything like this, we will obviously use the experiences of others as our guide. We want to know what to look for, what to expect, and we end up groping through our own subconscious preconceptions or the suggestions of others rather than being receptive to something new and different. Initially, meditation usually does not produce any radical phenomena in your consciousness. That is, the spiritual impressions you receive are often comfortable and always natural, yet you cannot adequately define them in relation to other experiences you have had.

The depth and intensity of the experiences increase as you become more receptive to moving deeper into an awareness of pure Being. There is never the slightest bit of danger involved, so you can feel free to move into the experience in a childlike, trusting way. I was informed by a student that a professor of a local university told his religion class that you could lose your mind through the practice of meditation. Unfortunately, this professor will probably never have the pleasure of finding out for himself and of speaking from his own experience on the subject, rather than from his own inaccurate speculations.

Sometimes the need to have an experience in meditation encourages the tendency to manufacture sensation in the body or flash colored lights across the screen of the mind. This probably stems from a kind of spiritual peer pressure that sometimes develops in groups of Truth seekers. Do not seek out such things. Genuinely noticeable changes evolve in time, and these sensations and lights are legitimate experiences, but they are not likely to occur with the beginner. The lack of these kinds of "signs" doesn't mean that your meditation is not productive. Every time you sit down to become still, you exercise your faith in the Invisible. You build a consciousness, laying up "treasures in heaven" that will eventually enable a conscious breakthrough into the higher realm of Spirit.

Finally, I want to include some thoughts on guided meditations and meditation music. While guided meditations (those led by other people) are popular and no doubt have their place, they often end up, as the dictionary suggests, as "a discourse intended to express its author's reflections." When someone tells me I led a good meditation, I'm tempted to say, "If you listened to me, then it wasn't a good meditation." Of course, I never do because I understand what they are saying. There are times when an external voice is comforting and reassuring.

Using guided meditations as a regular means of entering the silence, however, is a little like using training wheels to learn to ride a bicycle. Learning to ride with the wheels attached is one thing; learning to ride without them is another. You can easily develop psychological dependence on a voice coming through the loudspeaker or out of the tape player, to the degree that, without its presence, you cannot get past your own busy mind. I remember seeing a little boy zoom by on a bicycle equipped with training wheels. The funny thing about it was that the wheels were positioned so that they were not even touching the ground! The boy was able to ride a two-wheeler, he just didn't know it yet. You can meditate without an external guide, but you may not find that out until you become consistent in your efforts to try it.

The same can hold true with meditation music. It has its place, to be sure, but it is not necessary. If the music is pleasing to the senses, it may prove to be an obstacle on your journey inward, subtly binding you to the realm of the senses. It can also trigger memories of previous experiences that may serve as obstacles to having new ones. I believe the less paraphernalia you have, the better off you are. Your goal is to be able to enter a meditative state whenever you wish and wherever you are, without having to worry about finding a place to plug in your tape player.

There is a tendency in some persons to discount their ability to do new things without the aid of a "professional." This attitude can have a subtly degrading effect on your self-esteem, supporting the belief that you cannot succeed in your meditation endeavor without an aid of some sort. In many cases, the motivation behind popping a pill and plugging in a tape may be the same. I think the advice of Theodore Roosevelt is appropriate in this case. He said: "Do what you can, with what you have, where you are."[17] The truth is, you have the ability you need to successfully commune with God. In most cases, perseverance in practice will bear this out. The obvious bottom line in this area is that you must decide what works best for you.

❧ 4 ❧

The Meditative Posture

The practice of meditation is simple in terms of physical posture. A good position is to sit in a comfortable chair where the spine can be straight, feet flat on the floor, hands resting on your lap or on the arms of the chair. Another option is to sit cross-legged on the floor with your hands resting open in your lap. The object of the position is to stay awake while releasing all thought of the body. Lying down is not recommended, because you may fall asleep. Remember, the goal of meditation is not to achieve deep relaxation. This is more a by-product than the goal. The goal is to acquaint yourself firsthand with the pure essence of life before it is colored by your own thinking. Again, you are to be a beholder and an alert one at that.

Releasing all thought of the body means it is important to achieve a degree of physical relaxation. With most of us, the body has become like a spoiled child constantly begging for our attention, and we need to teach it to sit quietly while we experience communion. When you are comfortably seated, you may wish to close your eyes and take a few deep breaths. You may want to speak words similar to these, gently repeating them as you move deeper into a relaxed state: *I now relax and let go.* Release the tension in your body as best you can, being careful not to attempt to force it out, causing added, unnecessary strain.

As you relax, it is best to turn your thoughts inward. Turning your attention to the inner depths of your consciousness is a private experience and is difficult to adequately explain. "As Chuang Tzu said, 'If it could be talked about, everybody would have told their brother.' "[18] You can tell you are making progress, however, for your mind will begin to slow to a relaxing and clear pace. Do not attempt to stop thinking, for you will end up frustrated. In fact, it may be helpful to slowly repeat a thought such as this: *I now move deeper into the pure essence of Being.* Use any sacred phrase or centering thought that appeals to you. This will help focus your mind in the direction you wish it to move.

You may find your mind darting off in different directions. While this can be frustrating, you need not give in to discouragement. Bring your attention back and continue your movement inward. Charles Fillmore said he would get up and move about if necessary. You may wish to stand and stretch and walk around a bit if you feel the need. Then sit back down and make another attempt. If you use a statement like the one I suggested above, you may find it helpful to speak it aloud, or at least in a whisper. This helps to focus your attention in the right direction.

How much time should you spend in your meditation session? This is entirely up to you, but thirty minutes may be a good starting point. Sixty to ninety minutes may well be ideal and almost no one need spend more than two hours. There will be days when it will take twenty minutes to bring order to your mind. Your meditation time should be quality time, a time when you are wide awake and long enough after a meal when your body is not busy digesting. I would also suggest, as Charles Fillmore did, that you pick the same time every day, at least initially, for there is something about this regularity that strengthens the process. When your time is up (and you will know when it is), get up and go about your usual business.

꙳ 5 ꙳

Simple but Effective

These procedures may seem elementary at first because meditation has, unfortunately, gained an air of mystique. You may be tempted to feel this unpretentious method is far too simple to be effective. You may be tempted to run out and buy a bigger book on the subject, consult a meditation expert, or spend a hundred dollars on a meditation seminar. All these may indeed be helpful, but none of them can guarantee that you will be able to accomplish your end. All you really need to do is to *keep working* with these general guidelines, feeling your way through by trying things that suit you best. There is no easy or quick way. The less you stuff your head with complicated metaphysical formulas, the better off you are. While there is nothing wrong with exploring new material in whatever form it may present itself, a problem lies in thinking that the new material will do the work for you. Every New Thought minister has had the experience of observing a large number of prodigal children in the far country thrashing through the husks of one teaching after another, forgetting that "the anointing that you received from him abides in you, and so you do not need anyone to teach you. But as his anointing teaches you about all things, and is true and is not a lie, and just as it has taught you, abide in him" (1 Jn. 2:27). Commitment to a personal experience with God assures progress.

How quickly do you think you are supposed to get results from your meditation time? Would you expect to sit down at a piano a few times and then play a piece by Chopin? Of course you wouldn't. And yet, at the same time, never underestimate what does happen every time you expose yourself to the process of meditation. You do cover ground whether or not it is discernible. This became clear one day as I was attempting to meditate and was apparently having the same results as all the other times before: nothing was happening. I finally opened my eyes to arise and everything was different. Each thing in the room seemed to be an energy field, a living thing that had properties of a wondrous quality. This is difficult to explain and was certainly an unexpected experience. I believe all the experiences I had prior to this served as a preparation for this brief insight. We never really know what is happening when we turn to the Infinite.

❧ 6 ❧

Some Manifestations of Meditation

You may find that your early manifestations of meditation do not come during your time of meditation at all. You might notice that during the day, at an unexpected hour, you suddenly experience a sense of peace and clarity welling up within. Or you may feel an unexpected sense of gratitude. You may suddenly be taken by the beauty of a flower or the song of a bird. You may even have a healing of some sort. You may not initially connect these experiences to your time of meditation, but it will dawn on you eventually.

These small hints of change serve to increase your incentive to further explore the practice of meditation. Your increased sensitivity shows you that you live in a world quite different than you thought, and you become eager to find out more about it. What before seemed commonplace begins to seem miraculous. What seemed to be a bothersome personality becomes a messenger of God. These things serve as guideposts marking the way to greater self-discovery and providing evidence that you are on the right path. But let me caution you again not to look for these things to happen. Let them present themselves as they naturally will. There is no telling what form your experiences will take or how long it will take them to appear.

In time you will enter into the "secret place of the most High," as the Psalmist called it. It is that secret place where your individualized Spirit bubbles forth from the Fountainhead.

> I lie abstracted and hear beautiful tales of
> things and the reasons of things,
> They are so beautiful I nudge myself to
> listen.
>
> I cannot say to any person what I hear—I
> cannot say it to myself—it is very
> wonderful.
>
> —Walt Whitman[19]

There is simply no way to describe this place within you, but it is there and it is real. In fact, once you get a glimpse of it, your whole standard of reality will be changed. Many things you felt were important will gradually slip away, and many things you never considered important will become priorities. These words of Jesus will take on a whole new meaning: "Many who are first will be last, and the last will be first" (Mt. 19:30).

≫ 7 ≪

Expect Wonderful Things

What will happen as a result of your entering the secret place? The most pronounced result will be that you will begin to understand your true purpose in life. You will have answers to questions that have plagued you and others for a lifetime. You will know Truth when you hear it and know how to find it when it is not apparent. You may rise up to be a great leader in your chosen field, or you may continue your spiritual journey quietly and unassumingly. Expect wonderful things to unfold in a natural, harmonious way. When you are consciously empowered from "the secret place of the most High" you can be sure you are in for the time of your eternal life!

The important thing about the practice of meditation is to make it your experience. Learn to address the problems that confront you with the attitude that you are free to experiment. There may not necessarily be a right or wrong way to do it. The apparent obstacles before you have stood before all people who have attempted to enter the inner realms of consciousness. With persistence and patience you will succeed in attaining an experiential understanding of the process of spiritual unfoldment.

PART III

The Art of Prayer

❧ 1 ❧

Prayer and Consciousness

In the first part of this book we discussed the difference between your world and God's world. God's world, if you remember, is the underlying reality of Absolute Good that you seek to enter in your time of meditation. Your world is a product of your consciousness, which means that your experience in life is greatly influenced by what you believe. While the practice of meditation infuses you with new life, your experiences will still be colored by many of the limited beliefs you have held, which are not easily displaced by your new realizations of Truth. As Emerson wrote: "It is easy in the world to live after the world's opinion; it is easy in solitude to live after our own; but the great man is he who in the midst of the crowd keeps with perfect sweetness the independence of solitude."[20] A concerted effort must be made to accomplish "the independence of solitude" in the midst of a busy day and to build a consciousness suitable for sustaining a higher experience. Prayer is the tool that will enable you to do this.

For example, in meditation you may receive the realization that as a spiritual being you are totally unlimited. Yet, when you go shopping for a new dress or suit you may not look at what you like but at what you can afford. In meditation you had a realization of limitlessness, but in practice you are still operating from limitation. Why? Because you have programmed yourself to think within a certain budgeted image of yourself. You are responding to a subconscious idea of limitation that you have accepted and lived out of for so long you do not even realize you are acting out of it.

This is not to say, of course, that you are to spend more money than you have or to think you can tap into God's unlimited abundance with a credit card. This is a mistake that is made all too often by many on the spiritual path. Being a good steward by engaging in sound financial practices is an important aspect of prosperity. Spending beyond your means to give the appearance of prosperity and then struggling to pay for it later is not a demonstration of God's abundance.

In this vein, a young man explained to me that he had a well-paying job but he did not like it and wanted to quit. Though he had no other job to go to, he felt he had sufficient faith to let the "Holy Spirit" provide for him. Any suggestion of finding another job before he quit his present one was met with, "Wouldn't that be a lack of faith?" He quit the job. After a short period of time he came back to the church asking for a loan to pay his light bill. I had to refuse him because I, too, knew that the Holy Spirit would provide for him. It may not have provided him with what he wanted immediately, but it would provide him with something of much greater value in the long run—a lesson in good common sense!

The only reason we experience limitation is that we have habitually accepted self-imposed limitations to the point that they have become so much of our identity that we do not even know we are making decisions out of them. We must start building a consciousness of abundance through study, meditation, and prayer, and by changing the way we think when we do little things like entering a store. Do we run first to the sale rack? Why not look at the things we think we really want and begin to get used to the idea that these things are not necessarily good for us? We do not have to actually buy everything we want in order to expand our consciousness. Every time we become *aware* of a pattern of limitation and we *interrupt* that pattern of consciousness, we *advance* toward a more suitable overall demonstration of the abundant life.

My father shares an amusing incident that illustrates how ingrained patterns of consciousness can go undetected even though we think we are changing them. Early in his married life he was a traveling sales representative for a feed and grain company in northern Missouri. Along with a suit, the attire of a businessman in those days usually included a dress hat. My father wore one. One day, as always, he removed it from his head when he walked into a small-town cafe for lunch. When the waitress came to take his order, he noticed she was having to try very hard to keep from laughing. When she brought his order to him she was still having the same problem. In the meantime, he noticed others in the restaurant staring and snickering. He did not know what their problem was but assumed it had something to do with the fact that he was not from their town. Finishing his lunch, he paid the check and, hat in hand, went out to his car. When he glanced in the mirror of his car he noticed, much to his dismay, that although he had removed his hat, his hatband had come loose and stayed on his head! He was so used to the feel of the hat that he could not feel the band still on his head, even though he had removed the hat.

We become so comfortable with our limited perceptions of life that even though we think we are changing, something of those perceptions—like the loose hatband—remains. These perceptions are brought to the surface of our minds throughout our day, prompting us to act in ways that keep us bound within their limits. If we are to fully demonstrate the limitlessness of the new vision we receive in moments of inspiration, we have to become aware of these habitual perceptions and do things that will push us beyond them. The tool with which to begin changing these ingrained patterns of consciousness is prayer.

2

The Purpose of Prayer

We have now covered two important points: (1) as a spiritual being, your purpose is to express all the attributes of God in everything you do; and (2) the purpose of meditation is to bring you into direct contact with the attributes of God. Now, a third point is this: the purpose of prayer is to integrate the attributes of God into your consciousness which, in turn, will manifest as corresponding conditions.

We are to look at prayer as a consciousness-raising tool, not as a method of begging favors from God or even as a problem-solving device. This attitude could be a departure from many of the preconceptions you have about prayer; but then such preconceptions often limit the effectiveness of this important tool.

The Aramaic word for prayer, *slotha*, means "to set a trap" or "to make an adjustment." The meaning "to set a trap" carries with it the idea that prayer is an activity which prepares the mind to capture insights into the characteristics of God. While this carries some connotations worth considering, the definition "to make an adjustment" is the most fitting for our purposes here.

Prayer is the activity of adjusting your mind, in every situation, to the higher spiritual standard unfolding in you as the result of your spiritual development. It is a conscious effort to harmonize your mind with the Mind of God, making divine attributes a part of your conscious awareness. It is practiced in special times of quiet solitude as well as in day-to-day circumstances, in situations such as the shopping excursion mentioned above, the healing of an illness, or the attracting of the perfect companion. In Part Four, we will deal specifically with the practical application of prayer in various conditions in life. For now, we will discuss the nuts and bolts of the prayer process.

If God's world is perfect and yours is not, and your world is a projection of your consciousness, then the raising of your consciousness will naturally lift you above the level of the problems you are experiencing. When we ask God to straighten out situations, our focus is usually on getting God to change the conditions, not to change us. In our eyes, we are not the problem. The problem is out there somewhere. We want change as long as we do not have to change. But problem areas in our experience have a direct correlation to the level on which our consciousness operates. When the cause in consciousness is removed, the outer condition responds accordingly. Our problems are solved from the inside out, not from the outside in. Is this easy to put into practice? No, it is not. It is not easy to understand that the only place we can deal effectively with life and the challenges it offers is within the realm of our consciousness. Nevertheless, when this understanding begins to dawn on us, the world becomes our footstool rather than our taskmaster.

I counseled a woman who had felt since childhood that she had been a victim of the insanities of the world. Indeed she had been, but she began to grasp the truth that all the power those people in her life had had over her had been given to them by herself alone. She began to withdraw that power from them, rendering them powerless to make the choices of what she would feel and how she would experience her life. Difficult as it was for her to make this transition, it was beautiful to watch and rewarding to know that if someone coming out of such a negative condition in life could make that kind of progress by solving problems from the inside out, it could be done by anyone. This is the only way we can permanently rise above our problems.

❧ 3 ❧

The Nature of Consciousness

The importance of understanding consciousness obviously ranks high when you consider the impact it has on the quality of your life. The terms *soul* and *consciousness* are often used interchangeably in metaphysical literature. Charles Fillmore wrote: "In its original and true sense, the soul of man is the expressed idea of man in Divine Mind."[21] Your soul uses consciousness as the means by which it expresses itself, the "idea of man in Divine Mind," into the realm of manifestation. To bring forth the true representation of this perfect idea, the conglomeration of ideas that make up your consciousness must begin to reflect the true nature of the soul. To the degree that they do, the soul is "saved" from the problems imposed by mortal limitations.

The soul has the ability to form conscious thought according to the ideal it perceives in God, or it can form consciousness according to appearances in the outer world of manifestation. Jesus warned his followers about judging by appearances, for on the surface, things can be deceptive. This was brought home to me one Sunday in the greeting line after church. A young woman introduced herself to me and explained that this was the first time she had come to our church. As I often do, I asked her how she had heard about Unity. She said she saw my name and several messages on a bathroom wall! Hearing this, the associations my mind suddenly began to make produced some disconcerting effects, which were apparently showing up all over my face. I do not consider myself to be a paranoid person, but I was curious as to where this bathroom might be, so I asked her.

She explained, to my relief, that a friend of hers who came to my church had a bathroom that needed painting. Since she did not yet have the money for the paint, she began covering the wall with our Sunday morning bulletin covers. On the backs of these covers I write a short Truth message that goes with the talk I give on that Sunday. These covers served to remind her of Truth ideas and provided a makeshift way of fixing the ugly wall. How easy it is to be deceived by appearances! Of all the possibilities that had suddenly run through my mind, this one had not dawned on me. If the woman had not told me the story, I would still be wondering about all the bathroom walls of restaurants and gas stations in our area.

Fortunately, there is a less deceptive way to form consciousness, and that is according to divine ideals imparted through the deeper levels of the soul. When we focus our attention here, the potential splendors of God's kingdom are expressed in our lives. Because the soul can look to the outer or inner worlds and form consciousness from the material it finds in either direction, metaphysical Christianity teaches that the soul is *pivotal.*

Jesus gave us a good example of how consciousness is built in what has become known as the parable of the dragnet. He said, "The kingdom of heaven is like a net that was thrown into the sea and caught fish of every kind; when it was full, they drew it ashore, sat down, and put the good into baskets but threw out the bad" (Mt. 13:47-48). According to Charles Fillmore, fish in the Bible always represent ideas. Ideas are constantly being introduced into the "net" of our awareness. Some we choose to keep; others we throw away according to our understanding. The choice we make determines the quality of our lives.

Consciousness is the structure through which divine ideas imparted through the soul are made manifest. Divine ideas will remain unexpressed potential until we build a structure that will permit them to come forth. Divine order, for example, has existed forever because it is an attribute of God. This does not automatically mean, however, that divine order will be apparent in your life. You must have a consciousness of divine order for it to manifest in your experience. If your consciousness is continually centered in chaos, you will demonstrate chaos. Divine order is still available to you no matter what you are demonstrating because, being a characteristic of God, it is omnipresent. Before it will become a part of your life, however, a restructuring of your consciousness must take place.

The law of aerodynamics, like divine order, has existed forever, yet was not successfully demonstrated by humankind until Wilbur and Orville Wright created a structure through which the law could be made manifest. Neanderthal man had access to the same law that governed flight, though he was not conscious of such a law, at least not conscious of it enough to form a structure through which flight could be demonstrated.

In a much broader sense, Jesus demonstrated the principle of resurrection because he had built a consciousness capable of supporting the divine idea of eternal life. This idea is here for us all to incorporate into our consciousness, but we have to release the structure we have built that supports the idea of death and limitation. Jesus pointed out the accessibility of eternal life and the means by which we are to lay hold of it when he said: "Do you not say, 'There are yet four months, then comes the harvest'? I tell you, lift up your eyes, and see how the fields are already white for harvest. He who reaps receives wages, and gathers fruit for eternal life, so that sower and reaper may rejoice together" (Jn. 4:35-36 RSV). To "lift up your eyes" means to raise your attention to this higher ideal of life, accepting the truth that it is God's gift to you.

Because the human race has not yet fully understood how this medium of expression is to be ideally used, we have "netted" many ideas that do not allow the full beauty of the soul to be reflected through the consciousness. These are ideas that have been gleaned from the limited world of appearances rather than from the Truth of Being. As individuals becoming conscious of our divinity, we have reached a point in our evolution where we are beginning to bring our spiritual identity forward into our conscious awareness. The result is that we are being "saved" from many of the limitations that plague the spiritually unawakened souls in the world.

⫸ 4 ⫷

A Fall or a Rise?

There is a common belief that humanity once enjoyed a spiritually refined consciousness from which we "fell" because of sin. The source of this belief is found in the third chapter of Genesis. The writer was explaining, in the context of both his view of the universe and his rather anthropomorphic view of Yahweh (Hebrew for *Jehovah*), how people experienced an often limited and difficult struggle to survive. Man, in the writer's view, had become a threat to the powers of God and something had to be done before he became God's equal. "Then the Lord God said, 'See, the man has become like one of us, knowing good and evil; and now, he might reach out his hand and take also from the tree of life, and eat, and live forever'—therefore the Lord God sent him forth from the garden of Eden, to till the ground from which he was taken" (Gen. 3:22-23).

In the mind of the ancient Hebrew, Yahweh was responsible for everything, including any present condition of struggle and suffering. Life was harsh for the nomad, and followers of Yahweh would naturally want to know why He would allow His people to struggle and suffer so. The answer would obviously go back to the first man and woman, since life had been difficult for as long as anyone could remember. "Cursed is the ground because of you; in toil you shall eat of it all the days of your life; thorns and thistles it shall bring forth for you; and you shall eat the plants of the field. By the sweat of your face you shall eat bread until you return to the ground, for out of it you were taken; you are dust, and to dust you shall return" (Gen. 3:17-19). Because Yahweh loved His people, He would have to be justified in expelling them from the Garden of Eden. Disobedience was a good reason because everyone could understand how God could love His people and still punish them, as they did their own children. "Those who spare the rod hate their children, but those who love them are diligent to discipline them" (Prov. 13:24).

The story answers, from a Hebrew mythological perspective, the question Job asks but fails to answer: Why do the righteous suffer? People suffer, the story says, because they disobey the laws of God. This would then provide an incentive for people to obey the laws of God so suffering would eventually cease. On the *metaphysical* level this is a valid observation, which we will discuss in the closing pages of this book. It is the *literal* interpretation that has given us problems with our spiritual self-esteem.

How we view the cause of our condition as a race, and how we see the remedy to this condition is all-important. So the question to raise is this: Should we feel obligated to view the condition of humankind through this ancient Hebrew's eyes? Why do we have to insist that we fell from a higher state of being and are now working our way back to God? Can we not see ourselves as the breakers of new ground, the instruments of a Creator who is perpetually embarking upon new creative territory, and who is as perfectly willing to experiment with new, more successful forms of creation as we are?

Certainly the anthropological and archaeological records support such a premise, for they reveal a human species that is forever spiraling upward and onward. In view of their findings, it is extremely difficult for me to accept the concept that we fell from a beautiful, harmonious condition of conscious union with God to a simpleminded, physically primitive creature such as Lucy.*

Though there is much speculation about the existence of spiritually advanced ancient civilizations, there is no accepted scientific evidence that they were anywhere near as advanced as our present one. Today we print spiritually-oriented books by the millions and teach metaphysical principles—from pulpits, platforms, and radio and television broadcasts the world over.

From a more secular standpoint it is becoming increasingly common to hear doctors of the mind and body announce their recognition that people are spiritual, as well as physical and psychological beings. They are beginning to take the whole person into account, a fact that allows them to recognize causes of disease as the disorders of the soul they are, rather than just trying to patch up the symptoms. Though still in its infancy and still the exception in medical orthodoxy,

---

*Lucy is the name given to the earliest remains of the bipedal primate family (family that eventually led to the modern human) found to date. These remains are believed to be approximately three to four million years old.

this quiet revolution, linked with the technological advancements that have been made in medicine, could very well lead to a world where disease is increasingly uncommon. With doctors like Deepak Chopra, Bernie Siegal, and Andrew Weil (to name but a few), who are now able to freely articulate their enlightened approaches to the healing concept, such a condition has become less of a hope and more of a realization. Why this tendency to discount the wonderful present by somehow feeling we are not quite as good as we used to be?

What a fresh insight we are given when we abandon the path that leads back to where we supposedly came from and embark upon the one that promises new possibilities. Do we need to remain chained to the impossible task of trying to live up to something we once were supposed to have been? How can we solve the problems of today if we think they are the punishment for some act our ancestors committed in the dark and distant past? How much more sensible and freeing it is to realize that God has brought us up to this point, that now the human race may be expressing more of its innate potential than it ever has.

⤞ 5 ⤝

The Systematic Nature of God

It is apparent to even the most casual observer that Divine Mind carries on its forward movement not randomly, but systematically. Everywhere we look in nature, we see systems within systems in operation. We need to look no further than to our own bodies to see an example of this. We recognize the whole body as a system composed of a variety of subsystems. There is a cardiovascular system, a nervous system, a digestive system, a respiratory system, and so on. The leaf on a tree is a system operating within the branch system which operates within the trunk system. These are fed and supported through a root system. Earth is a system operating within a solar system which in turn is operating within a galactic system which is operating within an unfathomable cosmic system.

Because the scientific theories of the beginnings of our universe have, for the most part, failed to take any kind of "God factor" into account, science has postulated the beginnings of our universe as somewhat of an accident, the system somehow beginning after the material worlds were formed. From a strictly material perspective, this would appear to be the case. But we know that behind all manifestation there lies a support system of intricate laws and, when conditions are right, Divine Mind works through these laws to produce manifestation. Since the existence of this system of laws does not depend on its having a material counterpart any more than the existence of the laws of mathematics depend on having someone write them on a chalkboard, we can easily speculate that they were fully intact before any kind of systematic order was detected in the material realm.

It is much like the "miracle" of spring, when all the new life gushes forth into manifestation through the myriad plants and animals we see all about us. Where was this life force during the winter months? It was right there waiting for the conditions to become right, waiting to spring forth into physical manifestation. Our universe sprang forth from an existing system of laws when, some fifteen billion years ago, conditions became right to support a manifest representation of them and our universe came on the scene with a "big bang."

The movement of cosmic law from the realm of potential to manifest possibility has established orderly and systematic methods for carrying out creation. These systems (plant, animal, planetary, galactic, etc.), which have as their goal the attainment of unlimited expression, have been refined through the process of evolution to the degree at which they presently operate.

According to the dictionary, a *system* is a regularly interacting or interdependent group of items forming a unified whole. Since our consciousness is a regularly interacting or interdependent group of thoughts forming a unified whole, it can be classified as a system.

It has been pointed out that consciousness is the

medium through which we uniquely express the qualities of Divine Mind. Consciousness provides us with the same systematic means of self-expression God uses. Through consciousness, we first build a system of ideas that serves as a structural foundation supporting an eventual manifestation of our choice, whether it be in the form of health and vitality, success and prosperity, harmony in relationships, or all of these. Prayer is the means by which we change the ideas, the individual components of our consciousness system, to bring them into conformity with the accomplishment of our purpose.

❧ 6 ❧

Open and Closed Systems

Most astronomers agree with the theory that our universe is expanding. Where this expansion is leading is a question for debate, for we find at least two schools of thought here. One side believes the universe will eventually reach a point where, like a huge cosmic yo-yo that has come to the end of its string, it will begin to close in upon itself, ending in a cataclysmic finale. The other side believes the components of the universe will continue to move beyond their current gravitational pull and expand indefinitely. One sees the universe as a *closed system*, the other sees it as an *open system*.

In developing a consciousness system, our goal is to build one that will expand indefinitely, which I like to think is God's plan for each component of the universe as well as for the universe as a whole. In the thirteenth chapter of Matthew, it is interesting to find that Jesus compared the kingdom of heaven to a grain of mustard seed which, he said, "is the smallest of all seeds, but when it has grown it is the greatest of shrubs" (Mt. 13:32). In that same chapter he said, "The kingdom of heaven is like yeast that a woman took and mixed in with three measures of flour until all of it was leavened" (Mt. 13:33). Both parables carry the idea that the kingdom of heaven is a process of expansion, which is in keeping not only with the discovery of modern astronomy but with our intuitive knowledge that life without limits is possible to attain. All religious systems teach this Truth in one way or another. Even those who believe heaven is a place we go when we die depict it as a place where struggle and limitation are nonexistent. The main difference between traditional Christianity and New Thought in this area is that the former sees the limitless life as something that cannot be attained until we leave the earth plane, while the latter sees it as something we begin to attain now. That this possibility exists so universally in human consciousness and is profoundly displayed in nature's insatiable desire to expand and perpetuate itself through all its diverse species is evidence that unlimited expression is a cosmic goal being communicated to every component of the manifest world.

When we speak of reaching a state of perfection, we may think of having reached a somewhat static state in which all lessons would be learned and all growth accomplished. There is no such level of attainment in this universe, for we find with every apparent end there is a new beginning. In light of the expansive nature of the cosmos, perfection should be defined as a dynamic state which continually allows for further expansion to take place. If we were to look for the perfect marriage, for example, would we not look for the one in which the couple involved is still discovering new things about themselves and each other; where appreciation for one another is continually deepening and the sense of adventure still evident? And isn't the perfect career the one that contains no ceiling on achievement and continuously offers new and exciting challenges that serve to bring more of a person's potential into expression? This is, no doubt, why Jesus suggested we become as children. Children are in a dynamic state of growth and expansion. Unlike most adults, they have not yet defined their beliefs and capabilities and are able to experience a fuller, more spontaneous lifestyle as a result.

Perfection is not a condition to be reached, but rather a process to be involved in. As someone asked, "When is the tomato perfect, when it's green or when it's red?" It is perfect at all stages, as long as it keeps growing. In this light Jesus' statement, "Be perfect, therefore, as your heavenly Father is perfect" (Mt. 5:48), could be interpreted as, "Keep yourself in a continual state of expansion even as your heavenly Father is in a continual state of expansion." Where before we may have felt Jesus was giving us an impossible task, we now see that he was describing an attitude which keeps us on the cutting edge of the evolutionary process of the human race.

There are a number of ideas we could consider as necessary items for an open system of consciousness. Here are just a few:

- God is recognized as the unlimited Source of individual being.
- The true Self (individual identity) is seen as spiritual and eternal.
- The body is recognized as an important but temporary garment whose maintenance is not considered to be the object of existence.
- Each experience is seen as a potential opportunity for further growth and development.
- Evolution is a hallmark.

A closed system of consciousness would bear the following characteristics:

- The belief that God is a separate entity.
- Self-image is based on a mental/physical identity.
- The main object in life is to meet the demands of the body and intellect.
- Competition with others is seen as the necessary means of survival.
- Each experience is judged as either good, bad, or unimportant.
- Involution (a tendency toward selfishness and greed) is a hallmark.

Each of us will obviously bear characteristics from

both lists, which should not be a major concern one way or the other. The important thing is to be able to identify those components in your own consciousness that contribute to a closed, self-defeating system of beliefs and bring them into conformity with the laws that govern growth and expansion. The accomplishment of this is the true office of prayer.

❧ 7 ❧

Three Levels of Consciousness

Changing consciousness through prayer involves the conscious, subconscious, and superconscious levels of mind. The conscious level is our field of awareness. It is the part that is "conscious" of our surroundings, what we are thinking and what we are feeling. The subconscious level, as Charles Fillmore wrote, is "the storehouse of our past thoughts and experiences." This is the level where our mental habit patterns and our self-image reside. The superconscious level is that part of the mind through which new spiritual inspiration comes. It serves as our direct line to God.

The personal computer provides us with a model that may help to illustrate these three levels of mind.

The "screen" of the computer could be compared to the conscious aspect of the mind. It allows us to display the data with which we presently want to work. This data is called up from the "memory" of the computer. The memory is like the subconscious level of mind in which previously entered data is stored. The "modem" is the part of the computer that allows us, via telephone lines, to connect to any data base anywhere in the world. This can be compared to the superconscious level of mind that allows us to tap into the all-knowing Mind of God.

The limiting preconceptions that cause our difficulties reside in the subconscious level of mind. The Truth of Being we desire to experience is imparted through the superconscious level, that part of the mind that is open to the Infinite. In prayer, we deny negative subconscious preconceptions that make their way into the conscious mind and affirm inspirations that come through the superconscious level. The result is an overall elevation of the consciousness system. Denial is the mental and emotional releasing of negative, subconscious preconceptions, false ideas we have used as a basis for our personal identity, but which are not founded in the Truth of Being. Affirmation is the establishment in mind of the Truth of God as revealed through the superconsciousness.

❧ 8 ❧

Denial: What It Means

It has been mistakenly assumed that use of the word *denial* in our spiritual vocabulary is the same as our use of it in a social/psychological context. Actually the connotations are quite different, and misunderstanding this difference has resulted in a great deal of confusion. For example, when it is said that practicing alcoholics are in the "denial stage," we understand this to mean that they are refusing to acknowledge that they have a problem. They may think that they are doing just fine; it is everyone else who has the problem. Of course, this form of denial is not confined to the disease of alcoholism. Most chronic sufferers tend to see themselves as victims of either someone else's shortcomings or just plain old bad luck, and they categorically deny any involvement in the production of their dilemmas. This is *psychological* denial.

Spiritual denial means *release.* Using denial to deal with certain problems means you are to release the energy you have been pouring into the appearance. It does not mean you are to act as if it's not there. Like the alcoholic, as long as you refuse to acknowledge that you have a problem, you cannot do anything about it. This kind of denial is not allowed if you expect to make any headway on the spiritual path. You must be willing to take responsibility, not for every undesirable event that takes place in your life, but for what you do with that event in your consciousness. This choice is responsible for degrading or enhancing the quality of your experience.

❧ 9 ❧

Affirmation: What It Means

If denial is the activity of releasing a negative, subconscious preconception, then *affirmation* is the activity of *establishing* your mind in the Truth of God. When the soil is prepared through denial, the seed of good must be planted through affirmation. An affirmation is a conscious effort to bring the Truth of God into your awareness and then act from that Truth. It is an act of stimulating the inspiration which the growing awareness of your spirituality brings while you are involved in your day-to-day activities.

When spiritual possibilities begin to dawn on us, they are frail in the thundering noise of the day's activities. How quickly they pale into insignificant hopes when we re-engage our minds in the office or plant routine, when the kids come crying to us, or while we entertain the in-laws. And when trouble comes, how easy it is to become a seed sown in rocky soil (Mt. 13:5), whose root system is shallow and whose consciousness of Truth is quickly choked out by the cares of the world. These are the times when Truth needs to be affirmed, when we boldly stand up and say, "As for me and my household, we will serve the Lord" (Josh. 24:15).

You have to choose to bear witness to Truth. It's not just going to fall out of your consciousness and into your situation. You have to speak it out, if not verbally, then mentally and emotionally, until it becomes the power force in your consciousness. You have to dare to speak Truth in the face of all evidence to the contrary. Speak it to whom? To yourself!

ꙅ 10 ꙅ

Denials and Affirmations Through the Spoken Word

While the most effective way to initiate denials and affirmations is through the spoken word, it should be thoroughly understood that the words used have no power to change anything. There must be mental and emotional movement in the activity they suggest.

For example, if you are feeling fear because you are confronted with a situation that seems to jeopardize your job, you might make a simple denial statement like this: "I now release this fear." Feel yourself gradually releasing the sensation fear is producing, repeating the statement as needed to help you stay with the activity of release. Then follow that experience with an affirmative movement, verbalizing it through words similar to these: *God's perfect order is now established in this situation. I am at peace.* Again, do not just say the words. Feel the truth of the words. The moment you do, your prayer is answered. Although it can and does happen, this does not necessarily mean that the external condition will instantly change to your benefit. It means you have begun to set up a new cause whose effect will be the establishment of some greater good in your life.

Remember: The purpose of prayer is to raise your consciousness, not just solve a temporary problem. As you succeed in transforming the negative mental and emotional environment produced by fear into an environment of peace and faith, you will have done your part. God will do the rest.

While you may not know exactly what the outcome of the situation will be, you can know without a doubt that there has been a response to your prayer and that God is now at work establishing the perfect outworking of the situation.

If you find yourself slipping back into fear and doubt, repeat the process of prayer. The object is to continue keeping yourself in a high quality of consciousness—to continue expressing the attributes of

God while the greater good is being established in your experience.

❧ 11 ❧

Creating Denial and Affirmation Statements

In creating appropriate denial and affirmation statements there are three things to consider. First, you can expect denials and affirmations to produce immediate changes in your mind. The use of the word *now* can help induce change. Second, since denial is a release of the negative, and affirmation is designed to establish the Truth, it is helpful to include the words *release* and *establish* in your statements in the appropriate context. Third, you need to identify the mental and emotional conditions to be released or established for inclusion in your statement. For the sake of clarity and future reference, these three steps can be helpful:

1. Expect your denials and affirmations to produce immediate action in your mind (mental and emotional levels). Use of the word *now* is helpful.

2. Include the word *release* in your denials and *establish* in your affirmations as reminders of the kind of change you want to see.
3. Identify the mental and emotional conditions you want to release and establish.

Now let's take a look at how we might implement these three suggestions, considering first how they may be used in forming statements of denial.

❧ 12 ❧

Creating a Statement of Denial

The goal of denial is to achieve freedom from the bondage of negativity *on the level of your thoughts and feelings.* You are to release the condition itself. If you say: "I now release this condition of financial lack" and you look out and see it is still there, you may get discouraged. But if you say: "I now release this fear of the condition of financial lack," you can have an immediate experience of freedom from fear, which will ultimately be an external experience of freedom from lack.

Conditions exist in time and space, and it often takes time and space to change them. Consciousness, on the other hand, always operates in the now and can be changed in "the twinkling of an eye" (1 Cor. 15:52). In much the same way you see the brilliant flash of fireworks displayed against the night sky before you hear their booming report, so you will experience the release of limitation within your consciousness before you actually see it dissolve in your affairs. The use of the word *now* is most effective when you remember this.

Identifying the negative feeling you wish to release is accomplished by simply asking yourself what you are afraid of, angry at, or sad about, and why. The results of asking yourself these questions and seeking to come up with honest answers can sometimes produce surprising results. I talked with a young woman who was frightened, she said, because she thought her boyfriend wanted to break off their relationship. When I asked her why she was afraid, she said it was because she didn't want to lose him. In talking with her further, however, it became obvious that her feelings for him did not run that deep. In fact, her real opinion of him was that he was a "self-centered, egotistical, good-for-nothing, lazy bum!" She ultimately realized she was not afraid of losing him. She was afraid of being alone, which turns out to be quite a different story and a rather risky reason to keep a relationship going. Getting to the heart of the negative feeling requires healthy doses of self-honesty and a desire to put spiritual principles into practice. Only then can you effectively focus your prayer work on a specific target. Otherwise, you run the risk of praying amiss.

When you identify the negative feeling, a simple statement like this should be sufficient. "I now release this fear of loneliness (feeling of inadequacy, sense of loss, feeling of entrapment, fear of lack, and so on)."

When you make the statement, seek to let yourself experience letting go of the negative element. Never force this feeling; simply ease into it. An audible utterance of your denial statement may be most effective when possible. When not, a clear mental statement will do fine. When you make your statement of denial, give yourself a few moments to experience it and then speak it again if necessary. As you begin to experience the release of negativity, you are ready to move into the affirmative side of prayer.

✣ 13 ✣

Creating an Affirmative Statement

Forming an affirmative statement is similar to forming a denial. The major difference, of course, is that you are seeking to establish a positive state of mind rather than to release a negative one. Again, you are seeking immediate mind action so the word *now* will be useful. Instead of releasing something, you are seeking to *establish* something, so *establish* is a good word to include.

There are at least two ways to identify the attribute of God you seek to call forth. The first is to determine what is the opposite of the condition you are releasing. If you are releasing fear, you may want to replace it with love. If it is anger, forgiveness is in order. If it is uncertainty, divine guidance is what you seek.

The other way is to ask yourself how you would feel if the negativity were removed. Would you feel joyful? Relaxed? Peaceful? Prosperous? Identify the word or words that best describe what you are seeking to establish in your present situation. An affirmation would go something like this: *The love* (strength, enthusiasm, guidance, and so on) *of God is now established in my mind and heart. Thank You, God.*

Again, seek to experience the Truth of what you are saying. When you have attained a measure of Truth you affirm, your prayer is answered. Jesus said: "So I tell you, whatever you ask for in prayer, believe that you have received it, and it will be yours" (Mk. 11:24).

❧ 14 ❧

Pray Without Ceasing

To be effective, your prayer work may extend beyond these formal sessions and become nothing less than a way of life. You are always using the principles of prayer, saying "no" to some ideas and "yes" to others. The law of demonstration operates through your consciousness twenty-four hours a day. The key is to be conscious of what you are denying and affirming. You may be saying "no" to your good in more ways than you realize, and "yes" to undesirable conditions you would otherwise want to release. Effective prayer is not as much a matter of learning new techniques as it is learning to do what you are already doing with your mind in a more directed, intelligent way—developing a conscious rather than an unconscious relationship with the creative processes of God.

PART IV

Practical Applications of Prayer

≫ 1 ≪

Meditation and Prayer:
Two Sides of the Same Coin

As you have read in the preceding pages, meditation and prayer have been presented as two distinct sides of the same coin. The practice of meditation awakens you to the inner presence of God, putting you in touch with the divine desire to express through you limitlessly. Prayer enables you to carry God's desire for unlimited expression through your consciousness and into your body and external affairs. It is the tool you use to release the concepts in your consciousness that obstruct the divine desire for unlimited expression, and to establish ideas based on principles of Truth which allow further growth to occur.

Perhaps a visual illustration of the relationship between meditation and prayer would be helpful. In the following diagram, the vertical line on the left (a) indicates growth that occurs as the result of meditation. The horizontal line (b) represents growth in one's ability, through the use of prayer, to reflect in daily life the unfolding spiritual awareness of greater health, prosperity, and harmony that comes through the practice of meditation. The asterisk in the upper right-hand corner of the chart (c) represents the ideal balance we want to achieve in these two practices. A state of successfully managing our earthly affairs is generated by balance in developing our spiritual awareness.

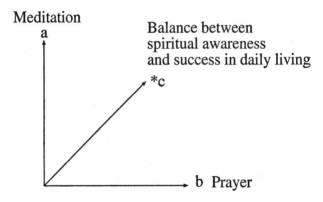

Many people become so engrossed in the practice of meditation that they cease to function well in day-to-day living. Or they use meditation as an escape mechanism to avoid taking responsibility for the condition of their lives. They tend to say very wise things of deep spiritual significance, but have a difficult time paying their bills.

On the other side of the coin are those who have adopted only the mental side of releasing the negative and affirming the positive, but have no consciousness of their spirituality. These people are most likely involved in the "positive thinking" movement and will have you hyperventilating with excitement ten minutes after you come into their presence; but they have little to offer in terms of spiritual enlightenment. We must successfully blend these two levels of development to the degree that our outer life fully reflects the beauty, tranquillity, and prosperity of God's infinite kingdom.

❧ 2 ❧

God, the Good

In your consciousness, your body, and your affairs, you are seeking to express more of God. You may not have called your desire for healing, prosperity, and harmony a desire for God, but that is exactly what it is. Perhaps by exchanging the word *God* for the word *good*, as someone has suggested, you can see it clearly.

All your endeavors have been centered around the attainment of greater good, whether for yourself, your loved ones, or your community. The good you sought may have been a healing of some sort, an increase in salary, a career, a spouse, or even a new car or home. But the motivation behind your search, past and present, has been and is the desire to experience greater good.

This desire for greater good is universal. One of Charles and Myrtle Fillmore's great teachers, Emma Curtis Hopkins, observed that even the lowly earthworm is infused with this desire. Every time an earthworm moves, it does so because it finds some benefit. Whether it be for safety, for food, or for pleasure, the motivation is always the attainment of greater good.

This universal desire for greater good is responsible for the harmonious orchestration of the diverse aspects of creation. Because we spring from the same source, and because God is responsible for providing us with the desire to expand, the achievement of greater good by each part always ensures improvement of the condition of the whole. We human beings, the only creatures who have the power to take matters into our own hands, are having to learn that success depends upon the success of our environment. We are finding that a clean environment, for example, is for our greatest good, that all facets of creation are so intricately interwoven that we cannot harm even the smallest aspect of nature without somehow harming ourselves. The more spiritually inclined we become as a race, the more clearly we see our unity with all life and the more we are concerned with the greater good of all. In this way the evolutionary process successfully spirals onward and upward.

❧ 3 ❧

God's Will

The question of God's will is a frequent puzzle to many persons on the spiritual path, especially as it concerns the acquisition of external things. Material gain, in and of itself, is not a bad thing. The problem is that we cannot extract any sense of permanence from this temporal realm. Any attempt to do so leaves us feeling empty and unfulfilled. We are to use our career choices, our relationships, and our creative ambitions as means of expressing the attributes of God, and we are in no way limited in the variety of ways this can be done. In creating successful channels (careers, relationships, and so on) through which these attributes can be expressed, however, we must follow the principles that govern their expression.

Time and again we have proved this to be the case. There is hardly a domestic plant or animal, for instance, that does not bear the marks of our selective breeding. Consider the rose. Chances are, every rose you have ever purchased was the product of hybridization. They are not simply natural products of God, but they are also the products of the human mind. Yet God sustains each of the thousands of new varieties because we have produced them in cooperation with the principles that govern their expression. Growers do not ask if it is God's will for them to produce red, pink, yellow, white, or purple roses. They know that as long as they work within the framework of the principles that govern the growth of the rose, they can produce any color they choose. In fact, there are approximately two hundred new varieties of roses produced each year.

So it is with you. It is God's will for you to attain unlimited expression through all you do. Success in whatever area you choose depends on how willing you are to develop the skills necessary to bring it forth. Are you willing to develop a consciousness that will sustain the manifestation you desire? Are you willing to devote the necessary time and energy it takes to develop your manifestation into a vehicle that will continually allow further growth and expansion to occur? In most cases it is not as much a question of God's will as it is a question of your willingness to do your part. This does not imply that the achievement of your desire has to come by the sweat of your brow. The implication is that it is necessary to keep your energies focused in the direction of your desires for as long as it takes to realize them. This is why it is important to pursue the things you love.

Do not think of God as one who deals out answers to your prayers as an all-knowing, wise father who knows what is best for each of his children. Think of God in much the same way you would think of electricity: Electricity does not question how it is used. It will run a blender, light a city, or heat a house. You make a choice as to what you want to "demonstrate" and then use the appliance that best addresses that desire. However, electricity operates according to certain laws, and the appliance must comply with these laws if it is to function properly.

In much the same way, you can express the qualities of God in any direction you choose as long as you comply with the laws that govern expression. In other words, your concern is not whether it is God's will for you to be an attorney, a banker, a scientist, a minister. Your concern is whether you are willing to do what it takes to sustain your career choice. Is it God's will for you to be a millionaire? God already sees you as limitless, so the question falls back on you. Are you willing to do what it takes to become a millionaire? Is it God's will for you to buy that thirty-thousand-dollar car?

What does Omnipresence care about cars? The question is: Are you willing to do what is necessary to buy that car?

You can demonstrate any kind of life you choose, but the rules of expression are this: First, you must build a consciousness for the thing you desire, and second, you must be willing to exert the effort necessary to bring it forth. Prayer is not a means of avoiding challenge; it is not a magic formula that will enable you to get something for nothing. Prayer is the means by which you build the consciousness that will successfully carry you through the challenge and into the manifestation of your choice.

ᱰ 4 ᱰ

Three Questions to Ask Yourself

Here are three questions you can ask yourself when trying to decide whether or not a particular vehicle of expression is right for you. Honest answers to these questions can provide you with some important guidelines toward your own success.

1. Do I have a natural affinity for this desire?

2. Have I made a deep commitment to develop my desire? Am I willing to pay the price by putting forth the necessary effort to succeed?
3. Will what I desire be of service both to myself and to others? Does this desire challenge me to be and express more of what I really am?

Let's think for a moment of some of the implications connected to these questions. The first one, "Do I have a natural affinity for this desire?" is important to consider. God's will for us is always first made known through our natural interests. Your will for greater freedom, prosperity, health, and harmony is the manifestation of God's will for you, and these things are best expressed when you do the things you love to do.

This does not mean that doing what you love to do will not have its challenges. It means you will be seeing the challenges as stimuli for growth rather than being resentful of having to face them because you do not like what you are doing anyway. A man who was facing controversy in his work reflected this resentful attitude when he said, "It's bad enough that I hate my job. Now I gotta put up with this stuff."

If all obstacles were removed from your life right now, what would you be doing? If you say you would like to quit your job and sit in front of a television set and drink beer all day long, you would quickly find that it is not what you really want out of life. You would find that it does not address your basic need to give or to make a contribution. What do you *really* want? The answers you get through honest reflection will be the things for which you have a natural affinity.

Too few people do what they really want to do. Instead, people do what they think they should do or what pays them the largest salary. But as Myrtle Fillmore wrote: "It surely is not wisdom and good judgment to keep at a thing year after year that brings no appreciable returns and that does not cause the soul to grow and expand and radiate through the body as ever-renewing health and youth. It is foolishness to devote oneself so wholly to a given line of action that one's own consciousness is neglected, so that one fails to learn how to keep in health and strength and how to bring forth the things needed for daily comfort and peace of mind."[22] If you do what you really love to do in life, if you pursue the lofty aspirations that well up from within the depths of your spiritual nature, the reward will be success on all levels.

"Have I made a deep commitment to develop my desire? Am I willing to pay the price by putting forth the necessary effort to succeed?" Many people fall short of achieving their desires because of the obstacles they come up against. But an obstacle is not necessarily a block on the path of success. It is often simply an indication that something on the present course has to change. That "something" could be some aspect of yourself: your attitude, your vision, your plan of action, your level of expectation. Teilhard de Chardin pointed out that "from the real evolutionary standpoint, something is finally burned in the course of every synthesis in order to pay for that synthesis."[23] Something has to change, something has to "burn" for us to get from where we are to where we want to be. Are you willing to continually seek until you find out what that something is? Or will you be satisfied by saying the obstacle is a message from God telling you your dreams are too good to be true?

Many people do not approach their dreams in a realistic way. They view them from a fantasy consciousness rather than one that understands the nitty-gritty of taking one practical step after another until the dream is realized. The attitude is often, "Oh, if this could only happen to me!" They look at their dreams as something God will bestow upon them someday when He finally notices what nice and deserving people they are. They do not see their dreams as a matter of building consciousness and taking the proper steps to make the dream a reality. As Emerson put it, "What will you have? quoth God; pay for it and take it—Nothing venture, nothing have—Thou shalt be paid exactly for what thou hast done, no more, no less."[24]

I remember talking to a woman who decided one day to become a country music singer because she had heard me say she could do anything she wanted to if she had faith and really set her mind to doing it. I am a musician myself, and it was obvious this woman had no natural affinity for music. She was suddenly struck by the glamour of being a singing star, wanted to experience a change in life to escape some difficulties she was facing, and heard her minister say it could be done. So, why not? Take a few voice lessons, sing at church a couple of times, maybe a club or two around town. By then a talent scout from a major recording label would hear her, put her in a recording studio, and presto! Next thing she knows she's another coal miner's daughter. It rarely works this way. You can learn to sing and sing well, but you will not necessarily succeed in the music industry on this virtue alone. There has to be a deep commitment to the business and all that it implies.

Years ago when I was struggling to make a living in the music business, I was told by a successful booking agent in Kansas City that actual talent is only about ten percent of the ingredients that make up a musical success. The rest are hard work, persistence, and business savvy. It is little wonder, in the field of the arts, that the term "starving artist" has become a cliche. God is the source of all good, but expressing that good through your life may also involve the development of marketing instincts and sound sales practices. We must not overlook this fact when we pray about anything.

"Will what I desire be of service to myself and to others? Does it challenge me to be and express more of what I really am?" The greatest service the accomplishment of any desire can provide is the challenge to grow. Likewise, the greatest service you can provide others is to somehow stimulate and aid them in their growth. This can be achieved in a variety of ways, whether you sell used cars, work in a factory, or hold public office. You can demonstrate Truth principles through your concern for the welfare of your customer, the quality of the job you perform, or a loving attitude in your work environment. Growth is taking place on all levels of consciousness and, therefore, all levels of service can be rendered toward the aid of humankind's development. Truth can be expressed through virtually any avenue you choose.

A man once told me that he thought my calling as a

minister was higher than his as a trucker. I said if he felt called to drive trucks, then my calling was no higher than his. I told him that we certainly needed truck drivers in this world and thanked him for doing the job.

Will your desire challenge you to *be* more, or do you desire it so you will no longer have to be challenged? If you want to make a million dollars so you can coast through the rest of your earth life, your desire will not be of service to you or anyone else.

❧ 5 ❧

Three Things to Remember

Most of the things we pray for fall into the categories of health, prosperity, and human relations. In praying for anything in any of these areas, we can summarize this section on God's will by bearing these three things in mind.

1. Your desire for greater good is really God desiring to achieve unlimited expression through you.
2. The vehicle you choose to express that good through is for you to decide.

3. Consciousness and a willingness to fulfill the laws of expression always precede demonstration.

Now let us see how we might apply these ideas in our prayer work in the areas of health, prosperity, and human relations, beginning with healing. Though we cannot hope to cover every aspect of these important areas, the examples given should provide sufficient guidelines for you to deal in depth with any variations you may be experiencing.

☙ 6 ❧

Healing

Your desire for perfect health has its source in God. Quoting again from Myrtle Fillmore's writings: "Whenever we have an experience of sickness, it is evidence that we have been letting go of our hold on the gifts of God. We have ceased eagerly to appropriate and analyze and assimilate and make use of the life of Spirit through our thoughts, our words, our acts, our living habits."[25] God is continually giving you the gift of health, and you experience that giving as the desire for health. In your time of meditation you will experience the Truth that God is whole, complete, without need of anything except to express through you as wholeness. The life signal of wholeness is being broadcast from the depths of your being and interpreted by you as the desire for perfect health. Your mind and body are the vehicles through which health is intended to be made manifest.

In your prayer for healings remember that prayer is primarily a consciousness-raising tool. Your first concern is not to heal your body, but to heal your attitude toward your body and toward any condition in your life that is prompting stress and limitation in your body. This means you are to lift your body image from one that is sick and weak to one that is whole and vibrant. To accomplish this, you are to deny or release your old body image and affirm or establish a new and healthy one.

As I shared this thought with a man who was experiencing a health challenge, he immediately saw how hard he had been working to heal his body. He was taking on a responsibility that was not his to take on. He realized he did not know how the immune system worked or how the cells cleansed and reproduced themselves. He found he was actually compounding the problem by forcefully visualizing the healing process as he thought it should work. This caused additional stress and frustration. Instead, he began simply to see himself as whole and free from disease. He allowed himself to trust God to do the work. He said his new attitude lifted a great burden from his shoulders and went a long way in helping to bring about his eventual recovery.

Begin your prayer "treatment" by sitting in a comfortable chair in a place where you will not be disturbed. While the prayer process can and will take place wherever you are, whether at work in the office or on the assembly line, walking down a busy street or driving the car, it is good to have special times of quiet focus in which you clearly see and experience your goal of wholeness. Relax your body for a few moments and establish the attitude that you are cooperating with the desire of God in your prayer for healing. It is God's will that you are healed.

With closed eyes, see your body as it is now. If there is pain or any undesirable sensation, bring it clearly to your mind. When you have done this, the process of release can begin.

⇛ 7 ⇚

The Healing Prayer

Form a statement of release in the manner described in Part Three of this book. It can be something as simple as, "I now release this from my life." Make this statement a few times, feeling the mental and emotional release gently occurring.

During the release process pay special attention to any strong impressions you receive. The image of a person or situation may come to mind, possibly as a signal to you that there is a need to release (forgive) them as well. Do not seek out such things, but if they come, include them in your releasing process or write them down for later treatment.

As you feel yourself releasing the limiting image, gently move into the affirmative side of your prayer. Following the guidelines previously given, form a statement similar to this: *God's perfect wholeness is now established in my mind and body. I am whole and free. Thank You, God.* Visualize God's perfect life filling every aspect of your body, and feel the delight and gratitude that naturally come with this vision. As you attain any measure of success in this transition from an unhealthy body image to a body image of wholeness, you can know something wonderful is happening. Do not look for things to happen. Let them present themselves to you in their own time. Just keep doing your part in prayer.

Along with your special time of prayer, be receptive to ideas that may come to you throughout the day. You may be inspired to enroll in an exercise program, attend a lecture on healing, reduce the level of fat in your diet, or any number of things. Trust God to *speak* to you on the level you can hear. Your daily work in meditation will also prove to be invaluable in becoming solution-oriented in this important area. The combination of these two practices of meditation and prayer will produce delightful results in the area of healing. Be dedicated to their practice and patient with yourself in learning to believe that you have received, even before there is evidence to indicate that your belief is sound.

%%% 8 %%%

Prosperity

Prosperity is a word generally assigned to the act of acquiring a surplus of money and material goods. While this certainly represents one facet of what we mean by prosperity, the demonstration of material wealth should be seen more as an *effect* of prosperity than as prosperity itself.

We have to define prosperity in the context of our true purpose. If our purpose is to express all the attributes of God in everything we do, then prosperity is anything on the spiritual, mental, and physical levels that assists us in carrying this purpose forward. In a spiritual sense, which is the foundation of its other aspects, prosperity begins when God is recognized as the infinite source of our supply. In a mental/emotional sense, we prosper every time we exercise our power to think and feel from the standpoint of our limitless spiritual identity, rather than from the constricted mind of the flesh. On the physical level, we prosper every time we move beyond some material barrier of limitation, whether that barrier is a low-paying, noncreative job; a restrictive income; an unhealthy body; a binding, unproductive relationship; or a religion that inhibits our spiritual growth through fear and condemnation. As the limitless attributes of God become a part of our consciousness through the exercise of our faith in God as our infinite source of good, the law of manifestation will clothe us with the material equivalent, the external side of prosperity. Jesus said it this way: "Strive first for the kingdom of God and his righteousness, and all these things will be given to you as well" (Mt. 6:33).

All the material possessions you seek are symbolic of spiritual qualities you wish to have. For example, the acquisition of money can represent a number of things—power, security, freedom, peace of mind—all of which are attributes of God. The acquisition of money alone does not mean you will obtain the spiritual qualities you desire. In fact, it is not unusual to see the acquisition of money have the opposite effect on a person: the more money that person makes, the more he or she may fear losing it, thus canceling out the effect of security, freedom, and peace of mind it was supposed to produce. The great American industrialist Henry Ford said: "If money is your hope for independence you will never have it. The only real security that a man can have in this world is a reserve of knowledge, experience and ability."[26] If you include the realm of spiritual matters in Ford's "knowledge, experience, and ability," you have the key to success on all levels.

The object of your prayer work is first to incorporate into your consciousness those attributes you feel your fulfilled desire will give you. Remember, consciousness precedes demonstration. If you know "the Lord is my strength" (Ex. 15:2), if you feel secure in the "everlasting arms" (Deut. 33:27) of God, if you experience the inner "peace of God, which surpasses all understanding" (Phil. 4:7), if you "know the truth ... [that] will make you free" (Jn. 8:32), then you have the necessary foundation of consciousness that will express as a life of great wealth. With this consciousness, everything you put your mind and hand to will prosper.

❧ 9 ❧

Expect Good Results, but Don't Limit Your Good to Expected Channels

As with the healing prayer, it is important that you refrain from the temptation to give yourself a prosperity prayer treatment and then go out looking for results. Now this doesn't mean you are to sit around and wait for things to fall into your lap. In everything you do, expect good results, but don't limit your good to expected channels. When you deal with infinite Mind, the number of channels through which your good can come is limitless, so practice being open to all possibilities. You might consider adopting the attitude of Lowell Fillmore, who said: "I go forth to meet my good." When you answer the phone, pick up your mail, drive to the grocery store, go to a job interview, have lunch with a friend, visit your doctor for a check-up, declare: *I go forth to meet my good.* See each activity you pursue as a potential channel through which greater good can unfold.

✥ 10 ✥

The Prosperity Prayer

As in the healing prayer, the prosperity prayer involves denial and affirmation. This time, however, as you are releasing images of limitation, you are establishing the sense of abundance and success.

If, for instance, you really like your job but it seems

your paycheck is inadequate for your expanding interest, the temptation may be for you to blame the boss for not giving you a salary increase in recognition of what a marvelous job you do. Or you may feel you've gone as high with this company as you ever will so it is time to change jobs. Either or both of these deductions may be accurate. You may ultimately have to confront your boss about your position, or you may end up leaving the company. But dealing with the situation from a prayer point of view does not start with the apparent issue. It starts with your consciousness.

Begin by identifying the negative feeling of limitation you think a raise or a change in jobs will overcome. To identify the negative feeling, it may be helpful to form and complete a statement like this: "A raise in my salary would eliminate this feeling of _____ _____." You may fill in the blank with a word such as *limitation, powerlessness, insecurity,* or *inadequacy.* Now put the word into a simple denial statement such as this: "I now release this feeling of limitation (powerlessness, insecurity, inadequacy, and so on)." When you are relaxed, speak your denial, seeking to experience the release of the negativity the words imply. When you have accomplished this, gently move into the affirmative side of prayer with a statement similar to this: *The infinite abundance of God is now established in my mind and circumstances. I am grateful for the perfect outworking of this situation for all concerned. Thank You, God.* Again, feel your response to this statement of Truth. When you are ready, get up and go about your normal business.

The results of your prayer work in this situation

could be anything from getting a raise, to changing jobs, to raising your attitude about the job, thus changing your relationship to it. You may feel moved to talk with your employer and explain how you feel. Perhaps your situation has come about because there is a need for you to learn to better communicate your needs through self-assertion rather than meekly standing by while everyone else decides what is best for you.

A man who felt he was a victim of his low-paying job and his world in general tried this method and found, to his surprise, that he was really a victim of his own low self-image. He said he was scanning his personal library one day and felt moved to pick up his copy of Emerson's essay "Self-Reliance." He randomly opened the book and these words seemed to jump out at him:

> Let a man then know his worth, and keep things under his feet. Let him not peep or steal, or skulk up and down with the air of a charity-boy ... an interloper in the world which exists for him. But the man in the street, finding no worth in himself which corresponds to the force which built a tower or sculptured a marble god, feels poor when he looks on these. To him a palace, a statue, or a costly book have an alien and forbidding air, much like a gay equipage, and seem to say like that, "Who are you, sir?" Yet they all are his, suitors for his notice, petitioners to his faculties that they will come out and take possession. The picture waits for my verdict;

it is not to command me, but I am to settle
its claim to praise.[27]

Suddenly realizing that his life was waiting for his
verdict, that people were only responding to the weak
and insecure man he was holding out to them, he
made a complete about-face. He realized that what he
thought and felt was important, that he did have
much to give, and that he need not be ashamed to give
it. Needless to say, as he began to express this attitude
through his words and actions, the waters parted, so to
speak, and he found a whole new and exciting way to
experience life. Having discovered new confidence and
self-respect, he found that others responded to him in
a totally different way. It was not long before he found
himself in a well-paid position of authority. In whatever way change comes about, it will come about, and
it will be for the highest good of all concerned if you
treat it as an opportunity, as this man did, to grow
spiritually.

Whether you are seeking to close a million-dollar
business deal, seeking employment, or seeking to
establish a clear understanding of the relationship
between the material and the spiritual realms, the principles of prayer work the same. The results you get
may be different than you hope for or expect, but if
you are sincere in pursuing your spiritual purpose, you
will find that everything works together for your highest good. Variation of your expectations may contain a
greater blessing than you originally sought. As you
continue your practice in meditation, your understanding of prosperity will expand to include aspects of

personal growth that have not even occurred to you. "No eye has seen, nor ear heard, nor the human heart conceived, what God has prepared for those who love him" (1 Cor. 2:9).

⟫ 11 ⟪

Relationships

Prayer can be used on behalf of another as well as to help establish better, higher quality relationships; subsequently, we will address these two areas separately. First, we will explore some possibilities on how we can pray for others for healing, guidance, and prosperity. Second, we will look at how we can use prayer to develop relationships in a personal, social, or business sense.

As with healing and prosperity, the most important aspect to consider with regard to relationships is our own consciousness. William James said: "Whenever two people meet there are really six people present. There is each man as he sees himself, each man as the other person sees him, and each man as he really is."[28] No wonder communications between people get muddled so easily! If we each could learn always to be true to ourselves in our relationships, we could cut through so many of the misunderstandings we have with others.

Probably the two biggest causes of conflict in relationships are: (1) we do not always say what we really mean; and (2) we do not always listen to what the other person is trying to say. Our prayer work concerning relationships should include both an effort to be diplomatically honest in saying what we mean and a concerted effort to listen to what others are saying to us. There is also a need to learn to accept others where they are without compromising the ideals we are trying to establish in our own consciousness.

❧ 12 ❧

Praying for Others

A question I'm often asked is, "In Unity, how do you pray for others?" This is an important question because there is a general misunderstanding about where our prayer work is to be focused. Some prayers for others are little more than attempts, with God's help, to impose our will on that person, rather than an honest desire to see their greater good established.

When we say, "I'm praying for your highest good," our attitude might really be "God, please help her see that what I am trying to tell her is right!" or "Please, God, Robert really needs that job at the bank. I don't see how we can make it any other way." We are not really trying to bring forth the highest good. We are trying to bring forth the highest good as we understand it.

It is also common for a person to pray for another with the true hope of gaining some good for him or herself. A woman called and asked for prayers for her son-in-law who was out of a job. She was "worried sick" over his predicament and wanted an answer for him so she could stop worrying. Of course we ended up praying for her condition first, for this is really what she wanted to resolve.

When we truly pray for others, we do not seek to alter their conditions, thoughts, or desires, no matter how negative or wrong these may seem to us. We seek to alter *our perception of others and their conditions.* If they are experiencing a health challenge, we work toward healing the negative image we hold of them. We release the image of them as sick or limited and establish an image of them as whole, radiant children of God. We do not ask if it is God's will that they be healed, and we do not concern ourselves with how their healing will come about. We simply, calmly know the Truth about them until, as far as we are concerned, they are healed.

When we behold a person as sick, confused, victimized, or weak, we are, in a very real sense, participating in the problem. This is not to say we are to turn our eyes from obvious facts, claiming they do not exist.

But if our goal is to bear witness to the Truth, we must begin by releasing the negative image we hold and bearing witness to what is possible. In a technical sense, our prayer for others is a prayer for ourselves. We release our limited image, an image which abides in our consciousness, and we establish an image of those for whom we pray expressing the wholeness of God. When we have achieved this, our prayer work is complete.

❧ 13 ❧

Ask Their Forgiveness

As a precondition to your prayer for others, it might be helpful to ask for their forgiveness. "Forgiveness for what?" you may ask. "I never did anything to them." Did you not form an image of them as sick, weak, limited, or fearful, needing your support? "But that is a fact," you say. Prayer does not deal with facts. It deals with *the establishment of Truth in your consciousness*. Ask, in the quiet of your mind, for forgiveness for having seen others in this limited way. See them responding positively and understandingly, telling you they know how easy it is to be deceived by appearances. Fully forgiven, you can begin your prayer treatment.

❧ 14 ☙

Attracting the Right Person

The other area in which prayer can be an invaluable tool is that of attracting and developing harmonious relationships. These can be relationships with people of the opposite sex, friends, business associates, people who share common interests, and so on. Perhaps by understanding a few simple ideas concerning relationships, you can avoid the experience of the disillusioned bride who, after one year of marriage, announced to her husband, "I took you for better or for worse, but you are a lot worse than I took you for."

A universal principle embraced by Unity is: Like attracts like. In terms of relationships, this means that you tend to attract to yourself people and conditions that reflect what you believe about yourself and what you expect out of life. Now this does not mean that you are directly and completely responsible for bringing every person you know into contact with you. Nor does it mean that you are personally responsible for creating every situation in your life. What it does mean is that you are responsible for the level of experience you have when you are with another or are involved in a particular situation you may be labeling negative.

For example, if you are involved in a relationship in which another person is taking advantage of you, you are allowing that level of relationship to exist and it is your responsibility to do something about it. Chances are, that person doesn't take advantage of everyone he or she relates to. There is a dynamic occurring for which two persons are responsible. You are not responsible for another's behavior. You are responsible for your reaction to their behavior, and your reaction to them determines the quality of your relationship. You have agreed to tolerate what you really feel is unacceptable behavior, and as long as you tolerate it, you will keep attracting it. In the most refined sense, then, it would be best to say that you attract the quality of the relationship you have with a person because of the standard by which you have chosen to operate.

The same holds true with circumstances. When facing a challenging situation many people ask, "What did I do to bring this on?" This is the wrong question to ask. The right question would be, "What is it in my own consciousness that is causing me to view this as a negative situation? Why am I having the level of internal experience I'm having, and what can I do to raise it?" This attitude makes effective prayer possible, for it places the possibility for change in the only place change can be initiated—in your consciousness and in the present moment.

⁓ 15 ⁓

Be Yourself

One of the secrets of developing productive, meaningful relationships is to become the kind of person you want to attract. Relationships are often sought for the wrong reasons. The premise many people operate from in developing relationships is this: I am an incomplete person so I must go out and find a person who has what I lack. When I find that person, together we will be a whole person.

Wholeness is an attribute of God and it is from within you that it must first be realized. If you do not have a consciousness of wholeness when you are alone, you will not have it ultimately when you are with another. A statement I always include in marriage ceremonies is this: "You are not entering this union (of marriage) because of what you lack but, rather, because of what you have to give." Whether the couples have the "ears to hear" at this point in their relationship I do not know. But it is a good attitude with which to enter into marriage.

In my own experience, which I feel is appropriate to share with you here, I found myself searching for that perfect person with whom I could share my life. I felt a kind of void that I was certain could be filled by the right person. In my study of Truth I eventually began to realize that I did not need someone else in order to be a complete person; I was complete in and of myself if I could just realize it. I stopped searching for someone else and began learning to love and accept myself and to be happy alone. In time I began to experience the wonders of self-love and acceptance, not in a selfish way but in a way in which I could appreciate myself as an expression of God. One day as I was sitting in church minding my own business, Beth, my then future wife, came in and sat right next to me! We were not two weak people who were brought together out of a mutual sense of lack and need. Our paths crossed because we both desired to learn how to express the best and highest that was in us. Our individual pursuit of this desire caused us to recognize each other when our paths crossed and is responsible for the beautiful relationship we enjoy today.

⋙ 16 ⋘

The Goal

The goal in your prayer to establish meaningful relationships is to first establish a meaningful relationship with yourself. In other words, your prayer work establishes in your consciousness those qualities that you feel you lack. Thus established, the principle of "like attracts like" draws to you a level of experience with others that is healthy and meaningful because you bring a consciousness of health and meaning into the relationship.

❧ 17 ❧

The Relationship Prayer

In forming a denial statement for your relationship prayer, it is helpful to ask yourself what you feel you lack as an individual. What problems will getting the right person solve? Are you battling loneliness? Insecurity? Lack of direction? The need to share experiences with another? These are all legitimate needs and certainly can be addressed in the right relationship. But they must be addressed in yourself first. Would you like a lonely, insecure person who doesn't know what he or she wants in life clinging to you? Of course you wouldn't, and neither does anyone else who is interested in developing a healthy relationship.

When you identify what you feel you lack, put it in your statement of denial. "I now release this sense of loneliness (insecurity, and so on)." As you speak these words, feel yourself let go of the negativity in the best way you can.

Create your affirmative statement according to what you want out of a relationship: *The divine qualities of security, love, and wholeness, are now established in my mind and circumstances. I am free to love and accept myself and to be all that I can be. Thank You, God.*

Feel the Truth of this statement and, as with all these types of prayer, seek to live out your denials and affirmations in daily life. Make a conscious effort to practice what you pray because prayer without practice is incomplete. God can do no more through you than He is doing at this moment, if you do not, in all ways, open yourself up to change. Look for that "perfect person" first in your own mirror. As an extension of your internal prayer work, make a practice of putting yourself in places that best represent the person you are becoming. As you build yourself from the inside out, it is only a matter of time before the people who are "right" for the person you wish to be will begin to appear.

❧ 18 ❧

A Few Final Words

In our practice of meditation and prayer it is important to bear in mind that there is an ebb and flow in our spiritual growth, times when no progress seems to be made and other times when we feel we are making great strides forward. Otherwise, when we hit occasional dry spells in our journey, we may feel like we are failing to make progress and become discouraged in our efforts to grow.

What is even more frustrating is our tendency to know the higher Truths but, through a kind of spiritual indifference, choose instead to cling to lesser ideals. Paul put it very bluntly when he wrote: "I do not understand my own actions. For I do not do what I want, but I do the very thing I hate" (Rom. 7:15). Who on the spiritual path does not understand well Paul's sentiments? Why, when we have seen grander possibilities for self-expression, do we continue to choose to be overrun by negative emotions, old limited thought patterns, and negative reactions to circumstantial appearances? What is it in us that keeps us hanging on to the old, spiritually degrading way of handling things when we know that the joy and freedom of choosing a higher perspective is just a thought or two away?

This question has probably plagued members of the

human race ever since it began to dawn on us that, while the surface of our being is very much involved in the finite world of expression, our essence is grounded in the Infinite. In one sense we stand with one foot in heaven and another foot on earth, and because we are in the beginning stages of spiritual development, we favor with attention our earthly standing over our heavenly one.

The Bible, as you might expect, addresses this tendency beautifully, and I think exploring it briefly might be a helpful way to bring this book to a close. Masked in the allegorical account of Cain and Abel, we find some helpful guidance in understanding this side of us that does what we "hate." We can also see how this seemingly negative allegiance to old values actually serves as a stimulus to push us into greater levels of expression.

✥ 19 ✥

The Attraction of the Familiar

Even though we may be on the inner path of spiritual awareness, we still have a tendency to gravitate to the familiar. We seek in people characteristics with which we can identify, circumstances we can predict, things that we already know. Most of us start our day with a routine which provides assurance that we will be off to a good start, and which allows us to follow a predictable path through the rest of the day. There is comfort and security in familiarity, a certain peace of mind, a sense of command and control that comes with knowing what to expect from one moment to the next.

Yet it is this tendency to seek out the familiar that is largely responsible for the mundane quality our lives sometimes have. If we are governed by it, life becomes dull and boring because our world becomes predictable. If we push ourselves beyond this tendency by constantly seeking to expose ourselves to new things, our experience broadens and our enthusiasm for growth increases. As we have previously discussed, life's nature is growth, change, and expansion. If there is one thing that is certain in life, it is that things are not going to stay the same for long. If we are not willing to learn to both initiate and to meet change successfully, we are bound to experience hardships and detours in our spiritual growth.

❧ 20 ❧

The Cain and Abel Dynamic

The allegory of Cain and Abel, found in the fourth chapter of Genesis, beautifully illustrates the inner dualism that both resists and welcomes change. The story demonstrates how these two opposing forces actually work to produce a higher state.

In reading the story, you know that Cain was a tiller of the soil—a farmer. Abel was a shepherd. The farmer must stay in one place, planting his crops in defined areas, making his location at any given time predictable. Cain represents that tendency in us to seek out the familiar, set up predictable routines, and hope nothing comes around to disturb our world. A shepherd, on the other hand, must constantly be on the move, changing the location of his flock so his sheep will not overgraze the land. Abel represents that part of us that is on the move, growing, indefinable, changing.

Characteristic responses to an unexpected turn of events by these two states of consciousness might go something like this: The Cain consciousness would ask, "Why did this happen to me? Why is it that things come along and mess up my nice, neat little world?" This consciousness constantly has to protect itself and its world from the fear of change. In contrast, the Abel consciousness would respond with, "Now I wonder what greater good is going to unfold through this situation. What lessons are there for me to learn that can help me to express a greater degree of my potential?" In other words, the Cain side reacts to protect its world, while the Abel side seeks creative, growth-producing action.

"In the course of time," the story goes, "Cain brought to the Lord an offering of the fruit of the ground, and Abel for his part brought of the firstlings of his flock, their fat portions. And the Lord had regard for Abel and his offering, but for Cain and his offering he had no regard" (Gen. 4:3-5).

In this passage we see the Lord, or the law of life and growth, favoring the gift of Abel and having no regard for Cain's. Taken literally, this can cause us to wonder why the Lord would show such favoritism. But spiritually interpreted, we see this is how life works. Life finds favor with the channels that are open to change and growth because, as I have already emphasized, its desire is to expand indefinitely. Abel represents such a channel in our consciousness while Cain represents that part of us that resists change. Life (the Lord) has many interesting ways of breaking down those channels that resist change.

Cain, displeased by God's rejection of him, kills Abel. We can, for a time, successfully protect ourselves from having to re-examine our parameters of thought and expression. We can repress the need to grow and expand in lines other than those of our habitual choosing. We can quench our ability to expand by convincing ourselves that we are consigned to operate within the specified realm of our past and present performances. But the law of life and growth urges us from within, asking, "Where is Abel your brother?" Life will not let us stay in our comfortable limitations for long. All efforts to keep from changing and growing are futile for, as the story goes on to say, Cain is banished to the land of Nod, which in Hebrew means "wandering."

What greater punishment could there be for one who thrives on familiarity and routine than to be made "a fugitive and a wanderer on the earth" (Gen. 4:14), to be placed in a situation where no known responses successfully address a change, where sense can be made out of a situation only after an expanded change of perception takes place? And yet this banishment, which comes in the form of apparently negative conditions, is only interpreted as punishment to that part of us that refuses change. God is too grand and loves us too much to allow us to confine ourselves to our limited definitions and plans for life.

This seeming punishment provides an explanation of why so many people suffer today. While the tendency of the race is to seek out the familiar and predictable, the nature of life is growth and change. Our resistance to growth and change does not bring them to a halt. The Cain side of our nature cannot successfully kill out the Abel side. We bring on suffering because we attempt to settle in to planting a permanent, predictable set of ideas when it serves us best to be constantly moving toward the greener pastures of a deeper understanding of Truth.

A man came for counseling who was obviously faced with this dilemma. He had taken a job in which nothing seemed right. The people he worked with were vulgar and had low ambitions. The hours he worked were long and hard. The job forced him to live a formidable distance from his fiancee, and this made planning their upcoming wedding extremely difficult. In short, his life was demanding more from him than he seemed able to give. He felt banished to "the land of Nod," a fugitive and wanderer. In Truth, however, his life was not demanding more from him than he was able to give. It was demanding more from him than he was used to giving. He was looking at these new developments in his life from the Cain side of his consciousness. He had "slain" the Abel side and could not, therefore, see any creative solution to his dilemma.

Because the Cain side of consciousness likes to deal in known quantities, it is always at a loss when previously unknown factors enter the circumstances. Since it is the defining, labeling, quantifying aspect of our consciousness, the Cain aspect defines and labels things "bad" when they fall beyond the scope of previous understanding and experience. Once a situation is labeled bad, it is attacked as an enemy, and the Abel side of our consciousness, the creative side, is slain. Change becomes the enemy and we do everything we can to keep it from occurring. In spite of our efforts, life pushes us out of our ruts and we are forced to face and grow through our fears of change. It is much better, however, if we learn to do this without being forced. Choosing our own method of learning is much easier than letting life choose it for us.

In his book *The Way of Transformation*, Karlfried Graf von Dürckheim writes:

Only to the extent that man exposes himself over and over again to annihilation, can that which is indestructible arise within him. In this lies the dignity of daring. Thus, the aim of practice is not to develop an attitude which allows a man to acquire a state of harmony and peace wherein nothing can ever trouble him. On the contrary, practice should teach him to let himself be assaulted, perturbed, moved, insulted, broken and battered—that is to say it should enable him to dare to let go his futile hankering after harmony, surcease from pain, and a comfortable life in order that he may discover, in doing battle with the forces that oppose him, that which awaits him beyond the world of opposites.[29]

This is a demanding view to be sure. But there is a great deal of Truth expressed in these words, for it is in the "dignity of daring" that all real growth is experienced.

The fear of change is a subtle thing and often we may not even know we are experiencing it. While the true office of prayer is to raise us up out of the Cain mentality, we sometimes use prayer to strengthen this mentality and keep it intact by asking God to remove the demands change is making on us. Most of us probably fear change because we think our good will be in some way threatened or taken away. But our real good can never be taken away. It is our interpretation of good that can be threatened. When life becomes centered around predictable plans, appointments, meetings, and identities, it quickly becomes a shallow and pointless experience. Soon we begin to think our routine is all life has to offer and we become slaves to schedules and concepts. It is quite easy, in this state, to become addicted to activity to the extent that if we don't have a busy day, filled with appointments and activities, we feel at a loss as to what to do with ourselves. Being alone makes us fidgety and depressed. While we may strive to achieve greater productivity, we are dogged by a certain sense of the futility of it all.

I remember reading an article in a science journal about a group of scientists who were trying to find out why moths fly around streetlights. What life-enhancing knowledge they had hoped to glean from this study I do not know, but the theory they came up with seems pertinent here. They proposed that the moth uses the moon as a navigational beacon and with the introduction of streetlights, the moth has become confused and uses the streetlight instead of the moon for its beacon. It begins by making very large circles around the light; these gradually become smaller and smaller, until the moth is flying frantic and pointless circles around a light that serves it in no productive way. So it is with us when we become "centered" in limited purposes and identities. We end up running in circles until we reach a point of complete frustration.

This is not as bad as it appears. It is often in these moments of frustration that we become most willing to examine our belief systems, to change old habits, to cut off those unproductive pursuits and ideas that do not bear the fruit of deep and lasting satisfaction we long for. Here we are forced into asking the most far-reaching questions, with the greatest implications toward freedom, that we can possibly ask: "What am I doing wrong? Why am I flying around this street-light?" Or, as the prophet Isaiah asks:

"Why do you spend your money for that
which is not bread,
and your labor for that which does not
satisfy?"
—Isaiah 55:2

Here we become willing to seek and surrender to God's higher purposes, to relax the strain produced by our blind groping for fulfillment that can only come from the spiritual plane. This does not necessarily mean we abandon our current involvements, though we may be led to make some major changes. We see that our purpose in life is to express our spirituality. The activities we undertake are determined by whether or not they contribute to growth in this direction. Charles Fillmore wrote:

There is in all the universe, including man, a balancing power of good, of perfection, which causes a readjustment, a healing, to set in after every transgression of the law, every wandering away from that which is whole-some and true.... Man seems ever to have wandered away to the limit; then a great reaction has set in, and he has been led back to a saner level. Thus he evolves, grows; and fi-

nally he shall come into a full consciousness
of his perfect good.[30]

The third son to Adam and Eve, Seth, is symbolic
of this "balancing power of good." He represents the
persistence of the true nature of reality asserting itself
through us. He is the voice of the prodigal son who
said, "I will get up and go to my father" (Lk. 15:18).
He is the voice of Walt Whitman singing:

> Long have you timidly waded holding a
> plank by the shore,
> Now I will you to be a bold swimmer,
> To jump off in the midst of the sea, rise
> again, nod to me,
> shout, and laughingly dash with your hair.[31]

We are involved in a mighty, upward, spiritual
movement, the scope of which we have yet to fully
comprehend. Our salvation does not lie in the practice
of protecting ourselves from the unfamiliar by becoming entrenched in predictable patterns of living that do
not allow changes to occur. Salvation lies in the inner
movement toward a conscious union with God, in
exploring new horizons that continually allow us to
expand toward becoming that "image and likeness" of
God we are created to be.

❧ 22 ❧

In Closing

I offer this work with the hope that you will better understand the forces working within you, that the occasional spiritual indifference, the seeming lack of progress, the feeling that you are sometimes losing instead of gaining ground are common feelings among all who have the courage to consciously step upon the spiritual path. Guilt and a sense of failure are debilitating when you work toward building consciousness, and they are bound to crop up from time to time if you do not understand these important dynamics of growth.

Meditation and prayer help you to consciously cooperate with the wonderful spiritual awakening you are undergoing. This Cain and Abel dynamic is an evolutionary process that occurs again and again, and you need to be patient with yourself as you learn (sometimes by groping in the dark) how it works. It is important to remember that the wisdom of God working through you knows how to lead you forward. It has brought you to this point. It will continue to carry you safely through all the interesting twists and turns in life, bringing you into a perpetual awareness of His full, everlasting, ever-loving presence.

References

References

Part I—Laying the Foundation

1. Walt Whitman, *Leaves of Grass*, The New American Library, New York, 1958, p. 195.
2. Laurence J. Peter, *Peter's Quotations*, William Morrow and Co., Inc., New York, 1977, p. 252.
3. Fred Hoyle, *Frontiers of Astronomy*, Harper & Row, New York, 1955, p. 304.
4. Kenneth F. Weaver, "The Search for Our Ancestors," *National Geographic*, November 1985, p. 579.
5. John Bartlett, *Bartlett's Familiar Quotations*, Little, Brown and Company, Boston, 1980, p. 140.
6. Newton Dillaway, *The Gospel of Emerson*, Unity School of Christianity, Unity Village, Mo., 1990, p. 65.
7. H. Emilie Cady, *Complete Works of H. Emilie Cady*, Unity School of Christianity, Unity Village, Mo., 1995, pp. 29-30.
8. Fritjof Capra, *The Tao of Physics*, Bantam Books, Inc., New York, 1977, pp. 180-181.
9. Whitman, p. 141.
10. Peter, p. 316.
11. Betty Edwards, *Drawing on the Right Side of the Brain*, Jeremy P. Tarcher, Inc., 1989, p. 4.

Part II—Meditation

12. Charles Fillmore, *The Revealing Word*, Unity School of Christianity, Unity Village, Mo., 1994, p. 179.
13 William L. Fischer, *Alternatives: New Approaches to Traditional Christian Beliefs*, Unity School of Christianity, Unity Village, Mo., 1994, p. 40.
14. Peter, p. 185.
15. Capra, p. 14.
16. Peter, p. 333.
17. Peter, p. 37.
18. Capra, p. 17.
19. Whitman, p. 311.

Part III—The Art of Prayer

20. Ralph Waldo Emerson, "Self-Reliance," *Emerson's Essays*, Thomas Y. Crowell Company, New York, 1926, p. 38.
21. C. Fillmore, p. 182.

Part IV—Practical Applications of Prayer

22. Myrtle Fillmore, *Myrtle Fillmore's Healing Letters*, Unity School of Christianity, Unity Village, Mo., 1986, p. 125.
23. Pierre Teilhard de Chardin, *The Phenomenon of Man*, Harper & Row, New York, 1965, p. 51.
24. Dillaway, p. 74.
25. M. Fillmore, p. 104

26. Peter, p. 438.
27. Emerson, pp. 44-45.
28. Peter, p. 317.
29. Karlfried Graf von Dürckheim, *The Way of Transformation*, George Allen & Unwin Ltd, 1971, pp. 79-80.
30. *Metaphysical Bible Dictionary*, Unity School of Christianity, Unity Village, Mo., 1995, p. 585.
31. Whitman, p. 92.

About the Author

J. Douglas Bottorff, ordained in 1981, has served Unity ministries in Kansas City, Missouri; Bay City, Michigan; Springfield, Missouri; and Evergreen, Colorado. Before moving to Evergreen, he served Christ Church Unity in Springfield for over eleven years.

In addition to writing this current book, Reverend Bottorff was a contributing author to John Marks Templeton's *Discovering the Laws of Life.* Doug has been writing articles for *Unity Magazine* since 1983. He also enjoys writing, performing, and recording music with a New Thought message. His cassette albums include *Let the Child Run Free, Life's Precious Call* and *You Are a Light.* He is working on a fourth, *Keep the Real Fire Burning.*

Doug is married to Elizabeth and is the father of a son and daughter, Ashley and Audrey.

108-1203-75C-9-95